John Edwin Sandys

An Easter Vacation in Greece

With Lists of Books on Greek Travel and Typography, and Time-Tables of Greek Steamers and Railways

John Edwin Sandys

An Easter Vacation in Greece
With Lists of Books on Greek Travel and Typography, and Time-Tables of Greek Steamers and Railways

ISBN/EAN: 9783337216542

Printed in Europe, USA, Canada, Australia, Japan

Cover: Foto ©Andreas Hilbeck / pixelio.de

More available books at **www.hansebooks.com**

AN EASTER VACATION

IN

GREECE

WITH

LISTS OF BOOKS ON GREEK TRAVEL AND TOPOGRAPHY
AND TIME-TABLES OF GREEK STEAMERS
AND RAILWAYS

BY

JOHN EDWIN SANDYS, LITT. D.

FELLOW AND TUTOR OF ST. JOHN'S COLLEGE, AND PUBLIC ORATOR IN THE
UNIVERSITY OF CAMBRIDGE

WITH A MAP OF GREECE, AND A PLAN OF OLYMPIA

Quacumque ingredimur, in aliqua historia vestigium ponimus
CICERO, *de Finibus*, v 2 § 5

London
MACMILLAN AND CO.
AND NEW YORK
1887

PREFACE

THIS volume contains a short account of a tour in Greece taken by my wife and myself in the spring of last year. The account is in the form of a journal, kept at the time for my own convenience only, and now printed with such slight omissions and additions as appeared requisite to render it suitable for another purpose. In preparing for our visit, we found ourselves hampered not a little by the want of definite and recent information on many points, which it was necessary to know while planning our route; and, since our return, it has occurred to me that any who are looking forward to a similar visit may find their labour lightened by the perusal of a journal showing, with some precision of detail as to times and places, how large a part of the country can be seen in the course of a short vacation. The journal also indicates what can be done by merely walking and driving, in the more easily accessible districts, without resorting to the intervention of a dragoman with his cavalcade of beasts of burden, carrying a complete canteen with beds and bedding and provisions for the way — a method of travelling, however, which, in the general absence of roads and inns, is still the only one available for seeing many portions of the interior. We spent a week very pleasantly at Athens, making excursions to Salamis, Eleusis, Phyle, Pentelicus, Laurium, and Sunium; and we afterwards visited Tiryns and Mycenæ, Nemea and Corinth, Delphi and Olympia, Zante and Corfu.

No one can be more conscious than myself how much was left unseen, owing to the shortness of the time at our disposal; and an extended study of the literature of Greek travel only increases this consciousness, while it inspires one with feelings almost of envy towards those who have been fortunate enough to have time for a more extensive tour. In *Appendix I*, I have drawn up an approximately complete list of all the books on Greek travel that have appeared down to the present time; and, in the case of some of the most important or most interesting, I have given an outline of the traveller's route. My object in so doing has been to direct the attention of future travellers to some of the best sources of information as to the various routes, and to facilitate reference to such sources. It is extremely difficult to make much use of such a mine of information as Welcker's *Journal*, without the help of a clue to its contents like that which I have tried to provide. I have also attempted to supply a classified conspectus of the literature of Greek Topography, and of some other subjects that are worth studying in connexion with Greek travel. In this part of my work I have had the advantage of using the carefully selected library of the Cambridge Museum of Classical Archæology, which includes that of the greatest of Greek topographers, Colonel Leake.

The map of modern Greece prefixed to this volume is intended simply to show the principal land and sea routes, and the lines of railway. Some information as to the best maps is given in *Appendix I*. However backward the country may unavoidably remain as regards ordinary roads, there are other means of communication that have been considerably developed and improved during recent years. Thus, there are railways now running from Athens to the Peiræus, to Laurium, to Kephisia; and also to Corinth, and past Mycenæ and Tiryns, to Nauplia and the site of the ancient Lerna. In August last, plans were submitted to the Government for a railway from Nauplia, by way of Tripolitza in the heart of Arcadia, to Kalamáta near the coast of Messenia. The approach to Olympia is now made easier by a short line from the port of Katákolo to the small inland town of Pyrgos, about a third of the distance to Olympia itself. In Thessaly, again, there is a line from the Gulf of Volo to Larissa, and also across some of the tributaries of the Peneios. And lastly, along the northern shore of the Peloponnesus, the railway is rapidly advancing from Corinth to Patras, having already passed the site of Sikyon and reached a village near the remains of Pellene. If its completion were unfortunately to supersede the steamers that now take the traveller through the splendid scenery of the Gulf of Corinth, it may be hoped that that magnificent approach to Athens will be restored again by the early opening of the canal across the Isthmus.

The mercantile enterprise of the Greeks has developed a considerable coasting trade by means of steamers stopping at all manner of places round the Peloponnesus and elsewhere; and the traveller can often advantageously resort to these means of communication. The first class cabins of the Hellenic Company, which has the largest steamers of the three Greek companies, are clean and comfortable, and afford better accommodation than can be obtained at any except the best hotels in Athens and Corfu. But the routes of these steamers, though duly recognised in Baedeker's *Griechenland*, are imperfectly known to English travellers in Greece. Thus, even so well-informed a traveller as Professor Mahaffy, in the recently published third edition of his interesting *Rambles and Studies in Greece*, is content to state that "a coasting steamer calls at Kalamáta every fortnight" (p. 6); whereas the Austrian Lloyd steamers stop there twice a fortnight, those of the Panhellenic and Gudé companies four times each, and those of the Old Hellenic eight times, making in all eighteen times a fortnight. Accurate information on these points is difficult to obtain, owing to the fact that, even in Greece itself, there is no publication containing in a collected form the time-tables of all the Greek steamers and railways. The tables of some of the railways in Attica are printed on a small card that can be got in Athens; some, but not all, of the railways are given in the Continental Bradshaw. Little beside the Thessalian line is included in Hendschel's *Telegraph*. The trains between Athens and Nauplia are from time to time advertised in the Greek newspapers; and only those between Athens and Corinth are mentioned in Cook's *Continental Time-tables*. This last publication, however, deserves credit for giving two or three pages of information about two of the three Greek steamer companies.

In *Appendix II* the time-tables of all the Greek railways and steamers are collected together for the first time. These tables have been derived from official sources, mainly from the placards and advertisements of the various companies, supplemented by information received in writing. In gathering together the material for them, I have had the special advantage of being assisted by two English residents in Greece, whose acquaintance I had the pleasure of making during my visit—Mrs. T. G. Dickson, of Athens, and

Mr. A. L. Crowe, of Zante—to both of whom my thanks are due for this and other acts of kindness. It is also an agreeable duty to thank Dr. Adler of Berlin for permitting the reproduction, on a smaller scale, of Dr. Dörpfeld's excellent plan of Olympia.

I hope that the information collected in this volume may be of use to travellers in Greece, and may induce some to visit that country who have hitherto been scarcely aware of the improved facilities for travelling which it now enjoys. If I succeed in this object, I shall be content to learn, without surprise, that they agree with Esmond in holding that "to see with one's own eyes men and countries, is better than reading all the books of travel in the world." But I trust that when, like the author of *Esmond*, they see rising around the olive-plain of Attica what he happily describes as a "chorus of the most beautiful mountains, the most elegant, gracious, and noble the eye ever looked on," their happiness may not be marred like his, when, on coming in sight of Sunium, he fancied he saw the Greek muse appearing to him in an awful vision, to reproach him with memories of his schoolboy days, when he had read her poets, but in fear and trembling, and had blundered through her histories. Rather may they rejoice with a joy unbroken, while they welcome, as the crown and consummation of the studies of the past, their earliest glimpse of the land where " the hills rise in perfect harmony and fall in the most exquisite cadences "—where " the sea seems brighter, the islands more purple, the clouds more light and rosy than elsewhere."[1]

J. E. SANDYS.

CAMBRIDGE, *March* 1887.

[1] Thackeray, Ed. 1877, vii 594-601 ; "A Journey from Cornhill to Cairo."—*Esmond*, chap. v.

CONTENTS

CHAP.		PAGE
MAP OF GREECE .	. *facing page*	1
I. CAMBRIDGE TO ATHENS .		1
II. ATHENS AND ATTICA . . .		5

    Pentelicus, 13; Eleusis, 19; Phyle, 31; Sunium and Laurium, 36

III. ATHENS TO NAUPLIA—TIRYNS—ARGOS—MYCENÆ—NEMEA—CORINTH .		42
IV. DELPHI. . .		66
V. THE ISTHMIAN STADIUM—CORINTH TO ZANTE .		84
VI. OLYMPIA		92
VII. ZANTE TO CORFU . . .		104
PLAN OF OLYMPIA . . . *facing page*		112

APPENDIX I.

	PAGE
BOOKS ON GREEK TRAVEL AND TOPOGRAPHY	113
Travels in Greece	113
Greek Geography and Topography—	
General	129
Special: Athens and Attica	130
Northern Greece	134
Peloponnesus	135
The Islands	137
Guide-books	138
Atlases, Maps, and Plans	139
Photographs	141
Flora	142
Manners and Customs, Folk-lore, etc.	142
Modern Greek	143

APPENDIX II.

		PAGE
TIME TABLES OF GREEK STEAMERS	.	145
Tables 1-4. Peloponnesian Line .		146-151
5, 6. Gulf of Argolis .		152-153
7, 8. Gulf of Corinth .		152-153
9, 10. Brindisi and Corinth .		154-155
11, 12. Ionian Islands' Line .		154-155
13, 14. Gulf of Arta .		156-157
15-19. Gulf of Volo		158-161
17. Syra and Laurion	.	159
20-25. The Cyclades .		162-163
26-28. Skyros. Epirus		164
AUSTRIAN LLOYD STEAMERS .		165-167
Table 29. Trieste—Patras—Salonica	.	165
30. Trieste and Constantinople		166-167
31. Peiræus and Syra .	.	166-167
32. Peiræus and Crete .	.	166-167
33. Trieste and Smyrna .	.	166-167

		PAGE
GREEK RAILWAYS		169-175
Table 34. Peiræus—Corinth—Nauplia		170-171
35. Corinth—Kamari . .		170-171
36. Athens—Kephisia . .		172
37. Athens—Peiræus		173
38. Athens—Laurium		173
39. Katakolo—Pyrgos .		174
40. Volo—Larissa		175

ERRATA

P. 145. *Routes to Greece* ; (2) *a*.
N.B.—The Steamers of the *Messageries Maritimes* have recently ceased to call at Naples, although advertised to do so in their own time-tables for 1887.

P. 129. To the list of *Books on Greek Travel* may be added: C. Engel, *Griechische Frühlingstage*, 8vo, Jena (Costenoble), 1887.

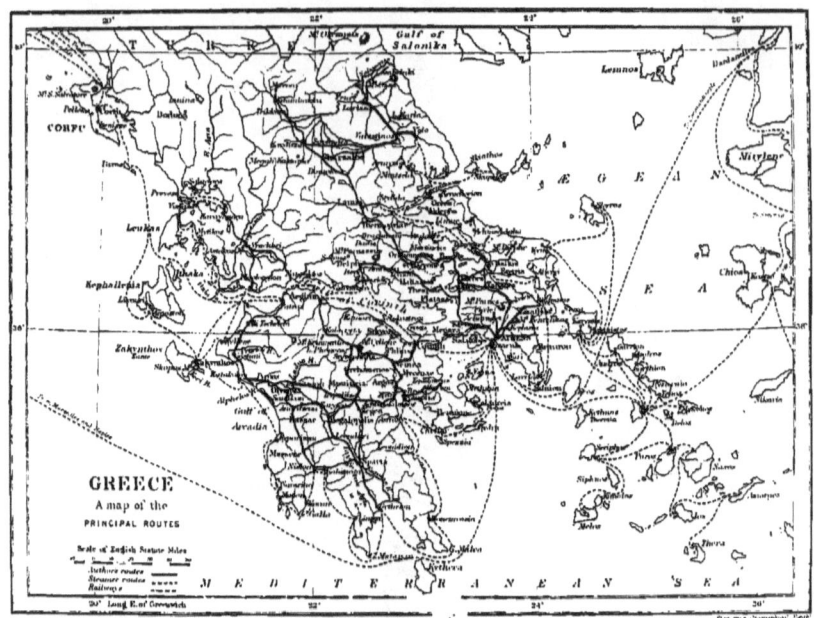

I

CAMBRIDGE TO ATHENS

χείματος ἠνεμόεντος ἀπ' αἰθέρος οἰχομένοιο,
πορφυρέη μείδησε φερανθέος εἴαρος ὥρη . . .
ἤδη δὲ πλώουσιν ἐπ' εὐρέα κύματα ναῦται
πνοιῇ ἀπημάντῳ Ζεφύρου λίνα κολπώσαντος.

MELEAGER in *Anthologia Græca*, ix 363.

The storms of winter now have passed away,
And spring's bright season smiles, with blossoms gay;
O'er the broad billows now the seaman sails,
The canvas swells with Zephyr's gentle gales.

IN the spring of 1886, undeterred by rumours of impending war between Greece and Turkey, my wife and I resolved on spending our Easter vacation in Greece. On March 17 we left Cambridge for Folkestone, crossed over to Boulogne the next morning, stayed in Paris for the night, and on the next day took the train for Marseilles. Beyond Lyons we had views of the Cevennes across the Rhone; and between Orange and Avignon, which we had visited a few years before, we saw the familiar cypresses standing out sharp and clear in the moonlight. It was past midnight when we reached our destination. During the next day we enjoyed the well-known panorama of Marseilles from the Church of *Notre Dame de la Garde;* and in the flower-market, a delightful place, where each of the saleswomen was sitting enthroned in a fragrant bower, we bought a box of oranges, in view of the long interval that on board the steamer divides the breakfast at ten from the dinner at five. At five P.M. we left for the Peiræus in the *Camboge*, a fine steamer belonging to the *Messageries Mari times*, and, as we slowly steamed out of the harbour, we saw around us all the neighbouring islands, including the one that is crowned by the memorable *Château d'If*. We had a comfortable cabin, next to the captain's, and excellent company on board in the persons of two Oxford travellers bound for the islands of the eastern Ægean. A Frenchman, who was going to Constantinople, was the only other saloon passenger, so that at dinner we formed, including the captain and the doctor, a party of only seven.

March 21.—A perfect day of bright sunshine and refreshing breezes playing over waters of almost unruffled calm. About one P.M. we passed through the Straits of Bonifacio, and had fine views of the serrated hills of Corsica and Sardinia, and of numbers of rocky islets, including Caprera, the home of Garibaldi. The day, 'most calm,' 'most bright,' recalled the story of the time when, in these very straits, John Henry Newman lay becalmed for a whole week in an orange-boat bound for Marseilles, and amid these islands wrote the lines beginning—

'Lead, kindly light, amid the encircling gloom.'

March 22.—About nine A.M., after passing the bold crags of Ischia and the low-lying island of Procida, we steamed into the Bay of Naples, and waited there till noon in full sight of Vesuvius, whose summit, however, was completely covered with clouds. The sky was perhaps less brilliant than on my former visit ten years ago; but the buildings along the shore, with their rich and varied colours, formed a pleasant picture; and, on leaving the bay, we had a delightful view of the villas of Sorrento crowning the southern cliffs, and also of the rugged heights of Capri, which remained long in sight before fading away like a cloud on the northern horizon.

March 23.—About four in the morning we passed through the Straits of Messina. I went on deck to look at the brightly lighted streets of the town, facing the dark Italian shore. We saw no more land that day.

March 24.—At half-past nine we came in sight of the Morea, and soon passed the bold headland of Capo Gallo and the misty mountains of Messenia, with all the grace of their varied outlines. About eleven we rounded Cape Matapan, where we looked in vain for the Greek monk who is said to emerge from his cell to give his blessing to every ship that passes by. Owing to the rough weather that is apt to prevail here, as it did in ancient times, it was not until two that we passed Cape Malea, leaving on our right the bare and rugged island of Cythera, which no one would have taken for a haunt of Aphrodite; indeed, as the French passenger remarked, she would obviously never have gone there if the Phœnicians had not taken her.

Not long after, the crag of Monemvasía, the home of Malmsey wine, was dimly seen on the Laconian coast; but, as the sky was overcast, the island of Melos was completely invisible. After a rather rough evening, we passed the lighthouse on the island of Hydra in the dead of night, and reached the Peiræus about one in the morning.

II

ATHENS AND ATTICA

ποῦ γὰρ . . . ὄψομαι . . . ἐκκλησίαν, . . . Κεραμεικόν, ἀγοράν, δικαστήρια, τὴν καλὴν ἀκρόπολιν, τὰς σεμνὰς θεάς, τὰ μυστήρια, τὴν γειτνιῶσαν Σαλαμῖνα, τὰ στενά, τὴν Ψυττάλειαν, τὸν Μαραθῶνα, ὅλην ἐν ταῖς Ἀθηναῖς τὴν Ἑλλάδα;   ALCIPHRON, ii 3 § 11.

MARCH 25.—The sky was brilliantly beautiful when we went on deck at seven o'clock, and, in the pearly light of our first Greek morning, saw the sunlit hills of Salamis. We were rowed ashore by two boatmen, who landed us at the custom-house, which happens to be on the site of a temple founded by Conon in memory of the battle of Cnidus; and, after going through the formal ceremony of walking past the courteous officers of the customs, we were soon driving along the five miles of dusty road to Athens, catching one or two glimpses of the Acropolis on the way. At the farther end of the long Street of Hermes, which runs from the Theseum and the railway station on the west, to the Royal

Gardens and the Square of the Constitution on the east, we found our hotel, the *Hôtel des Étrangers*, looking out upon the green trees, which are a relief to the eye after the glare of the surrounding streets. An excellent room was ready for us, and we arranged to stay for a week, paying a sum equivalent to £1 a day for both of us, this charge including lodging, meals, and attendance.

After breakfast we started out on our round of sight-seeing among the ruins of old Athens. We began with the *stadium* on the Ilissus. During the voyage I had come across the short description of it in Pausanias, and had been struck by the ambiguity of his language, which leaves it almost an open question whether it is the upper end of the *stadium* or the upper part of the stream that resembles a crescent in shape. The former is his real meaning.[1] The *stadium* was one of the works that marked the financial administration of the orator Lycurgus; but part of the substructure alone is now visible, and the slopes that gleamed with seats of white marble in the days of Herodes Atticus, are now green with

---

[1] I 19 § 7, ἄνωθεν ὄρος ὑπὲρ τὸν Εἰλισσὸν ἀρχόμενον ἐκ μηνοειδοῦς καθήκει τοῦ ποταμοῦ πρὸς τὴν ὄχθην εὐθύ τε καὶ διπλοῦν : *i.e.* From a point above the Ilissus, a hillside, of the form of a crescent in its upper part, descends in two parallel lines to the bank of the river.

grass and bright with poppies of a deeper than wonted hue.

We wandered back to the Ilissus, and walked along a narrow path on its left bank, under a row of small plane-trees, with the tiny stream of clear water flowing beside them, and recalling the well-known description of the scene of Plato's *Phædrus*. After descending the stream for a short way, we reached the fountain of Callirrhoe, which gushes out of a low wall of rock between two pretty cascades.

We next visited the ruins of the Olympieum with their lofty Corinthian columns; and, after passing through the arch of Hadrian, and threading a very narrow lane known as the Street of Tripods, we soon reached the Choragic monument of Lysicrates, a small and elegant structure in the Corinthian style, somewhat spoilt by poor surroundings. Then, by a poverty-stricken approach, grandly called the Street of Dionysus, we made our way to the Great Theatre, and there we rested for a while on some of the upper seats, looking across the Saronic Gulf to the purple slopes of Ægina, rising in graceful outlines to a summit about 1730 feet above the sea. Descending to the lower seats, I reached the centre of the foremost row, and enthroned myself in the marble stall reserved in ancient days for the priest of Dionysus. From this point I looked across the orchestra at the sculptured reliefs of Dionysiac legends on the frieze of the proscenium; we then crossed the foundations of the successive walls of the buildings of the stage, and found the altar of Dionysus standing among ruinous fragments, far removed from its proper place in the centre of the orchestra. It is distinctly broader and more bulky than the slender copy of it which was recently made for the Greek plays at Cambridge.

We then examined the interesting remains of the temple of Æsculapius on the south side of the Acropolis, with its colonnade and its sacred fountain, and stayed for a while in the Odeum of Herodes Atticus, the seats and many other portions of which are in fairly perfect preservation. After this we struck across the road to the south, and soon reached the summit of the Museum Hill, which is crowned by the monument of Philopappus, and commands a splendid view of Ægina and Salamis. Both of these islands we saw to perfection, and much more besides, for beyond them extended the mountains of Argolis, while to their right there arose the massive crag of the Acrocorinthus, and in the distance the snowy summit of Mount Cyllene in Arcadia, more than seventy miles away. After this glorious view, we cared but little for the so-called prison of Socrates, or the fabulous tomb of Cimon, which are excavated in the rocks of this hill. So, after a passing glance at these, we pressed onward up the slope of what is commonly known as the hill of the Pnyx.

Here, on the open hillside, lies the great semi-circular space where the assemblies of the Athenians are supposed to have been held. The upper part of this space is bounded by a low wall of rock, near the middle of which is a small stone platform ascended by steps, which inscriptions now in the British Museum have caused to be identified as the altar of *Zeus hypsistos*, but which is still regarded by many as the *bêma* of the Athenian orators. A bitterly cold wind was blowing from the north as I stood on this inclement spot, watching the strands of cloud streaming down as of old over Parnes.[1] The passing shower in which we were soon caught was sufficiently uncomfortable to make one applaud the good sense of the apparently superstitious rule which broke up the

---

[1] βλέπε νυν δευρὶ πρὸς τὴν Πάρνηθ'. ἤδη γὰρ ὁρῶ κατιούσας ἡσυχῇ αὐτάς . . . . χωροῦσ' αὗται πάνυ πολλαί, διὰ τῶν κοίλων καὶ τῶν δασέων.
ARISTOPHANES, *Nubes*, 324.

assemblies of Athens at the fall of the first drop of rain.[1] On such a day as this, even if a Demosthenes had been able to speak, it may well be doubted whether any one could have stopped to hear him.

To the north-east of the hill of the Pnyx lies the Areopagus. Scrambling up the steep steps cut in the native rock, we soon attained the narrow platform round which the elders sat in judgment under the open sky, with the accuser and the accused seated before them on the two white ledges called the 'stone of relentlessness' and the 'stone of outrage.'[2] In point of extent the platform was better fitted for the pulpit of St. Paul than for the court of the Areopagites; and a far more ample space in the adjacent rocks is assigned to the cave of the Eumenides.

From this gloomy cavern we ascended along winding paths, fringed with aloes, to the vast remains of the Propylæa, turning aside to linger awhile over the exquisite temple of the Wingless Victory, and then advancing along the route of the Panathenaic procession towards the graceful Erectheum, and the majestic Parthenon with its weather-beaten columns of Pentelic marble mel-

---

[1] διοσημία 'στιν καὶ ῥανὶς βέβληκέ με.—AR. *Acharn.* 171.
[2] Pausanias, i 28 § 5.

lowed by time into marvellous hues as of gold or amber. In the museum of the Acropolis, which was fortunately open, we saw the recent finds—seven female figures, including several representations of Athene with the well-known archaic smile, as well as a quaint and diminutive Aphrodite.[1]

On descending from the Acropolis we visited the Theseum, the most perfectly preserved of all the Athenian temples. But, on this occasion, we only walked round it, reserving the interior for another day, and then returned by the Street of Hermes to the hospitable doors of our hotel.

March 26.— In the morning I went to the Ionian Bank, where I learned from the courteous manager that, at the literary club called the *Parnassós*, the paper for the evening was to be on a purely agricultural subject; that Parliament was no longer sitting; that, owing to the prospect of war, the University lectures were suspended; and, lastly, that (as an alleviating circumstance) a circular note for £10 was worth as much as 311 drachmas in paper money, instead of about 250 in silver.

Opposite the Bank, in the fine Street of the Stadium, I saw the stately Parliament House;

---

[1] Some of these have since been photographed in Part I of *The Museums of Athens*, by M. Cavvadias.

and, in a still finer street running parallel to it, the sober and substantial structure of the University buildings; and next to these, the Ionic façade of the modern Academy, with statues of Athene and Apollo before it, and a gilded frieze around it—a gleaming fabric of white marble, whose splendour remains unsullied in the pure air of Athens. In the same quarter is the house of Dr. Schliemann, with the name ΙΛΙΟΥ ΜΕΓΑΡΟΝ in large letters of gold on its front, and with groups of memorable statues ranged along the roof.

In the afternoon we went to Salamis. At one o'clock we entered the train for the Peiræus, reaching it in twenty minutes; walked across the head of the harbour, and then struck off a little to the right, to gain the straits beyond an intervening headland. On our way we were detained by a shower, and were kindly invited to take shelter in a rude little hovel, where a man and his wife and their four little ones were cowering round a brazier of hot ashes. The perfect politeness of these poor people was remarkable.

Starting afresh, we hastened along a muddy road to the bay of Keratsina, and then by the shore below Mount Ægaleos, till we reached a point beyond the ferry by which Salamis itself is approached. The ferry is about two hours' walk from the Peiræus. All this while we were enjoying ever-varying views of the familiar landmarks of the memorable battle, the bare islet of Psyttaleia, the tapering promontory of Cynosura, and the hills of Salamis almost closing the entrance into the bay of Eleusis. Beside all these, we had splendid prospects of Ægina and the coast of Epidaurus, and even of the Acrocorinthus and Mount Cyllene.

At 4.45 we hastened back, and succeeded in reaching the Peiræus in time for the 6.30 train. On arriving at Athens and alighting at the station near the Theseum, it was not without a passing shock of surprise that I heard myself greeted for the first time by some eager Athenian cabmen with the Greek equivalent for 'A cab, Sir?'— ἅμαξα κύριε! ἅμαξα κύριε!

March 27.—Our excursion for the day was the ascent of Pentelicus. At half-past nine we started in an open carriage, leaving the hill of Lycabettus on our left, and passing through Ampelokípi (the *deme* of Aristeides and Socrates), just before reaching the open country. After a few miles of very tolerable road, we turned off to the right along a rough track with deep ruts that made our carriage jolt again and again in a most distressing manner, till we reached the village of Chalandri, where all the dogs came out to bark at us. The remainder of the road is far better, winding gradually uphill till it reaches the monastery of Mendéli, or Pentelê, near the foot of the mountain, an hour and a half's drive from Athens. On our way we passed numbers of vineyards and olive-trees, while by the roadside there were green slopes of sward, brilliant with hundreds of purple and crimson anemones. It must have been flowers like these that prompted the poets of old to give glowing epithets like φοινικάνθεμον to the bright season of spring.[1]

At the monastery there was some building going on, but we failed to find a monk to guide us to the summit. However, our driver, who was a handsome young Greek with a well-bronzed complexion, got an intelligent quarryman, who was looking after some blocks of marble in front of the monastery, to show us the way. We began our walk about eleven o'clock, and, after crossing some plantations on comparatively level ground, went steadily up the hill along paths that were strewn with shining fragments of marble, and

---

[1] Pindar, *Pyth.* iv 114, φοινικανθέμου ἦρος ἀκμᾷ, and Meleager quoted on p. 1, πορφυρέη φερανθέος εἴαρος ὥρη. Tibullus, iii 5, 4, and Columella, poët. x 256, *ver purpureum*.

across little lawns that were carpeted with bright anemones, till the flowers became fewer and fewer, and the ascent increasingly rugged. Toward the south-west the familiar panorama of hills and islands began once more to disclose itself, and Salamis, Ægina, Epidaurus, and the mountains of the Morea came into fuller and fuller view. We paused for a while near the ancient quarries in front of a low cliff of solid marble, scored with the names of modern Greeks and Russians carved in massive characters. To our right was a large cavern with graceful festoons of maiden-hair and gleaming stalactites falling from its roof; and in its floor, in a square basin of marble, a small pool of clear cold water. Our guide was a quiet and unobtrusive companion, with a gentle and kindly politeness in all that he did, and with an enviable power of sustained endurance in climbing up the roughest of paths. I followed him for a little way into the darker and colder part of the cave, without caring to respond for long to his repeated invitation: πήγαινε κάτω, πήγαινε κάτω ('Come down!'). To the right, just outside the cave, was a small chapel carved out of the rock with a shrine fitted up with an altar, and a ceiling decorated with Byzantine frescoes. This was about half-way. After struggling on over blocks of stone and branches of stunted brushwood, we reached a point of outlook from which we had our first view of Euboea, with its rugged hills rising beyond the narrow straits. From the same point we looked down for the first time on the battlefield of Marathon, bounded on the land-side by its fringe of low hills, with the road to Athens running between them, and closed toward the shore by the crescent-shaped bay, familiar in all the maps and plans of the battle. The battlefield, in the words of Byron, 'preserves alike its bounds and boundless fame.'

On reaching the summit, 3640 feet above the sea, we sheltered ourselves from the cold blast behind some rude stone walls, and enjoyed the full magnificence of the panorama. To the north was the finest point of all, the snowy pyramid of Mount Dirphys in Euboea rising to the height of more than 5000 feet. Towards the south and south-east, among the many islands now in sight, were several of the Cyclades, Andros, Tenos, and Ceos, with some of the smaller islands off the Cape of Sunium, which was itself hidden from view by the hills of the mining district of Laurium; while to the north-west, among the villages of Attica, we saw close at hand the hamlet of Tatoi near the famous fort of Deceleia, which guarded the most eastern of the passes of Parnes. Immediately below us to the north, we looked down once more on the field of Marathon. According to Pausanias (i 32 § 2), there was a statue of Athene on Pentelicus, probably on the actual summit; and it can hardly be doubted that it was from the crest of this very mountain that the gleaming shield was lifted up, which was supposed to have been displayed by the Alcmæonidæ as a signal to the Persians immediately after the battle (Herodotus, vi 115).

At 2.30 we began to descend, and at about 4.30 reached the monastery, having taken about five hours in all. After an *al fresco* lunch rather late in the day, we started back at 5 o'clock, and found the anemones, which had looked so bright as we came, already closing their petals for the night. The strong cold wind of the morning had given way to a warmer air, while we watched the sun descending in a sky of pale amber behind the delicately purple hills as we returned to Athens.

March 28.—We went up Lycabettus, which rises to the height of 919 feet, north-east of Athens, and has a distant resemblance to Arthur's Seat near Edinburgh, though it is much more bare and rocky. The prospect from the summit includes the best general view of Athens, in which the Acropolis, rising to 350 feet, is naturally the most central and prominent object. To the left of the Acropolis lies, in the middle distance, Ægina. To the right of the highest point of that island is the lofty peninsula of Methana; then, the mountains of Argolis, and, to the right of the Peiræus, the straits and hills of Salamis, the lower spurs of Mount Ægaleos, with the snows of the distant Cyllene; and, lastly, to the right of this, the nearer mountains of Megara and the range of Parnes.

After enjoying this view from the seats of stone in front of the chapel of St. George, which gives the hill its modern name, we descended by the path between the two peaks of the hill and struck across the northern part of Athens to the ' Central Museum ' which lies, as it happens, on the circumference of the city. Here we saw many statues of the highest interest, among the best of which was the Hermes of Andros; also a great number of beautiful marble vases carved in low relief, like the Grecian urn of Keats's ode,

> ' With brede
> Of marble men and maidens overwrought,'

and many other funeral monuments, several of which had the figure of a winged siren above them. It must have been some such figure as this that was placed, we are told, over the tomb of Isocrates. At the far end of the museum there was a copy of some remarkable paintings of birds and grapes, discovered in a tomb at Corinth in 1882.

In the afternoon we paid our second visit to the Acropolis; and then sat out on the Museum Hill, enjoying the view of Ægina and the coast of Epidaurus.

March 29.—We rose early, and, after walking to the wrong station, succeeded in catching the train to Eleusis at half-past seven. It is possible to walk there in four hours by the direct route over the Pass of Daphne across the range of Mount Ægaleos; but the intervention of that range compels the railway line to make a considerable *détour* and to go inland, through the olive groves of the Cephisus and along the Attic plain, for at least seven miles, till it reaches the small village of Epano-Liósia, a little to the west of the site of Acharnæ. It then crosses one of the depressions in the above range, taking about an hour in all to reach Eleusis.

At the station we found an old and feeble pensioner, the custodian of the ruins, awaiting the train. We went with him through the village, passing on our way many gaily dressed Albanian women clad in blue and red striped with gold, some of them carrying on their shoulders large water-vessels of rough pottery of a simple and elegant shape. On reaching the ruins, we passed through the shattered fragments of the greater and lesser Propylæa, the former resembling in plan and dimensions the Propylæa of the Athenian Acropolis, and the latter being a far smaller structure only thirty-two feet in breadth. Among the broken remains of this, I observed two separate portions of an inscription bearing the name of [APPIVS · CLAVDI]VS · AP · F · PVLCHE[R], a name that recalls the passage in Cicero's letters where he states that his predecessor in the pro-consulship of Cilicia is proposing to put up a πρόπυλον at Eleusis.[1] With the help of the old *custos* I put the pieces together again for the benefit of future visitors; but inscriptions of such interest and importance ought on no account to be allowed to lie scattered about on the ground among broken bits of ancient buildings.

Beyond the inner Propylæa we passed the

[1] Ad Atticum vi 1 § 26, audio Appium πρόπυλον Eleusine facere. The inscription was discovered in 1860, and is printed in the *Corpus Inscriptionum Latinarum*, i p. 181, [Ap. Claudi]us Ap. F. Pulche[r] propylum Cere[ri et Proserpi]nae cos. vovit [im]perato[r coepit] etc.

spot where, until the year 1801, lay 'the colossal bust of Pentelic marble, crowned with a basket,' which is now in the Fitzwilliam Museum at Cambridge. The inhabitants had an almost superstitious regard for this piece of ancient sculpture. On days of festival they used to burn a lamp before it; and, when Dr. E. D. Clarke purchased it from the Turkish governor of Athens, they declared that the ship which carried it off would never get safe into port,—a prediction which was actually verified by its being wrecked and lost near Beachy Head.[1] The bust was once supposed to be a fragment of the statue of Demeter herself, but, as observed by Leake, 'it seems rather to have been that of a Cistophorus, serving for some architectural decoration, like the Caryatides of the Erechtheium.'[2]

We soon reached the remains of the great temple of Demeter, the most interesting portion of which was the place of assembly, where the worshippers sat on seven rows of seats cut out of the solid rock on three sides of a long quadrilateral. It was probably here that the initiated saw the various symbolical representations connected with the Eleusinian mysteries. For any minuter

---

[1] Dr. Clarke's *Greek Marbles*, pp. 33-37.
[2] Leake's *Athens*, ii 161.

particulars we turn in vain to Pausanias, who closes his very curt account of Eleusis with the tantalising remark : 'a dream has forbidden me to write of the things within the wall of the sacred enclosure : to the uninitiated it is not permitted even to make inquiries concerning them' (i 38 § 6).

After visiting the custodian's cottage, and examining the contents of the adjacent shed, which is used as a museum for some of the smaller pieces of sculpture, we went a few steps upward to the acropolis of Eleusis, where we sat down for a while, enjoying the view of the hills of Salamis, which here resemble a series of natural fortifications guarding the bay. Where these hills dip down to the west, the mountains of Argolis come into view ; while near us, on our right, are the two little peaks known as the *Kérata*, which crown the most southerly spurs of Cithæron, and mark the boundary between Attica and Megara.

At one o'clock my wife left for Athens by a train that moved so slowly that a dog accompanied it for some way, barking vigorously at it. Meanwhile, I walked back to Athens by the Sacred Way over the Pass of Daphne. Soon after leaving Eleusis, which was crowded with cavalry in connexion with some military manœuvres, I passed the massive remains of a Roman bridge, with wild flowers growing in profusion over its arches, and with an ancient well before it, and two Albanian women, one of them in a bright costume, drawing water from the well. After a dusty walk along a road, which for a while kept at some distance from the bay, and showed frequent signs of severe inundations, like those mentioned in the speech of Demosthenes against Callicles (§ 28), I reached some small lakes of salt water of a brilliant green and blue—the ancient *Rheitoi*—and soon after gained the shore of the bay. From beyond this point, the view, as one looked back, was even finer than that from the Eleusinian acropolis. It included a retrospect of Eleusis and of its beautiful lake-like bay, shut in on the south by the varied outline of Salamis; while, above it, there came into full view the Geraneian mountains beyond Megara.

At the point where the road turns off for Athens, I sat down for a while in the verandah of a deserted house, where I was shortly joined by a Greek peasant with a gun slung across his shoulder —happily a peaceable person—from whom I got the modern names of some of the flowers I had gathered on the way. The answer one usually receives on these occasions, is that the flowers are called λουλούδια; but, as that is only the generic name, the reply is useless. He gave me the name of κιρκάσι for the star of Bethlehem, and ἀγριοκρίνα for some purple irises.[1]

On reaching the top of the pass, I visited the monastery of Daphne, where I waited for some time in a desolate courtyard, until an old man came and opened for me the door of the church. The interior of the cupola is embellished with Byzantine mosaics, which were much damaged and blackened by the smoke of candles, and were really hardly worth waiting so long to see. While walking down the hill I had a fine prospect of Pentelicus, and soon after reached the view of Athens which is celebrated in the pages of Chateaubriand.[2] At the present time, however, the effect of Lycabettus and the Acropolis is marred by the white houses of modern Athens, though the olives of the Cephisus still form an effective foreground to the picture. After roaming onwards to the south of the 'groves of Academe,' I lingered for a time among the palms and cypresses of the desolate and dismal botanical

---

[1] *Iris Sisyrinchium;* Sibthorp's *Flora Graeca,* i 30, fig. 42. I cannot find the name κιρκάσι in the ordinary books of reference.

[2] *Itinéraire de Paris à Jerusalem,* p. 186-7 of the English translation, ed. 1812. Henri Belle, *Voyage en Grèce,* p. 52.

garden, and at last reached the *Dipylum* and entered Athens, returning to the hotel by streets which bore the famous names of Euripides and Praxiteles.

March 30.—We visited the old and new cathedrals, which stand side by side in an open space near the Street of Hermes. In the new cathedral, which is elaborately decorated, the most interesting object is the tomb of the unfortunate patriarch Gregory, one of the victims of the Greek war of independence. The old cathedral was far more interesting. It is a very small building on the site of the *Serapeum*, with many ancient reliefs imbedded in its outer walls. Shortly afterwards we entered a small church which bears the singular and much-disputed name of Kapnikarea, standing in the middle of the Street of Hermes. Its low domes give a picturesque effect to its external appearance, but in the interior there was little that was worth seeing except a recent mural painting representing its reputed foundress, the beautiful and talented Empress Eudocia. We then proceeded to the Central Museum, where we spent some time in viewing those of the sculptures which we had missed on our former visit. Among the minor objects of interest were some curious specimens of ancient devices for measuring out liquids; a number of cavities of various sizes scooped out of a flat stone, with a small hole at the bottom of each to let out the liquid when measured. After this we visited another museum called the *Polytechnikon*, a beautiful building of Pentelic marble, where we saw the antiquities found in the tombs of Mycenæ, and an admirable collection of Greek vases.

In the afternoon we went, with a lady residing in Athens, to see some of the ancient remains to the north of the Acropolis, the 'Tower of the Winds,' the 'Gate of the Oil-Market,' and the 'Stoa of Hadrian.' The last of these was, until recently, buried at a level of twenty-five feet beneath the bazaar of Athens; but a fire had fortunately swept away much of the flimsy fabric of the bazaar, and made it possible to explore the ancient building. They were busy with the excavations at the time of our visit, and numerous inscriptions had recently been brought to light. We next went through a curious narrow street, the shoemakers' market, which was gay with long rows of bright Albanian slippers of scarlet leather, 'with the toe turned up in front like the prow of a gondola.' All this quarter was particularly picturesque and delightfully quiet, and we were loth to leave it for the gloomy and grimy and noisy street of the blacksmiths. After a while, however, we were gladdened again with the sight of the Theseum ; and spent some time pleasantly in examining its frieze, and in viewing the interior, in which is preserved the well-known sepulchral monument in low relief, called the *Stele of Aristion*, sometimes spoken of as the ' Warrior of Marathon,' but now generally ascribed to the time of the Peisistratidæ.

After this, my wife returned to the Theatre of Dionysus, to make a sketch of the upper rows of seats, with Ægina in the distance, while I went on to the remains of the *Dipylum*, which separated the inner from the outer Cerameicus, and to the adjacent ruins of the Sacred Gate, which led out to the Sacred Way to Eleusis. These remains, which were excavated about 1876, lie in a large open space of waste ground considerably below the level of the surrounding soil. The ground-plan of this neglected part of the outskirts of the town, though marked with singular clearness in the maps, was really rather difficult to disentangle, owing partly to changes caused by the winter rains ; and the surroundings were too unsavoury to allow of one's lingering long over the attempt.

It was pleasanter to turn to the adjoining Street of Tombs, excavated at various dates between 1861 and 1871, and forming part of the ancient cemetery of the Cerameicus. Among these I saw the sarcophagus of plain marble bearing the name of Hipparetê, the wife of Alcibiades, and others of far higher artistic interest with admirably designed reliefs, representing, in a style of quiet and chastened reserve, the tender scenes of parting, in which the living members of a family bid farewell to the dead.[1] Different from these, and even of higher interest, is the monument of Dexileôs, which was discovered in 1863. The youthful hero is represented on a rearing charger, thrusting his lance into the prostrate form of a warrior who has fallen back on his shield under the prancing legs of the horse, and is vainly endeavouring to parry the thrust. Below the relief runs the following inscription :—

>Δεξιλέως Λυσανίου Θορίκιος·
>ἐγένετο ἐπὶ Τεισάνδρου ἄρχοντος·
>ἀπέθανε ἐπ' Εὐβουλίδου
>ἐγ Κορίνθῳ, τῶν πέντε ἱππέων.

>Dexileôs, son of Lysanias, of Thoricus,
>Born in the archonship of Teisandros,
>Died in that of Eubulides
>At Corinth ; one of the five horsemen.

---

[1] Mahaffy's *Rambles and Studies in Greece*, chap. iii, p. 62-72, ed. 3.

This is a rare example of a dated Greek epitaph; Teisandros was archon in 414 B.C., and Eubulides in 394, the year of the battle of Corinth. 'The five horsemen,' says Mr. Newton, 'must have distinguished themselves by some signal prowess of which history makes no mention.'[1] The Greek historians, indeed, do not throw any direct light on this incident. From Xenophon's *Hellenica*, iv 2 § 17, we learn that the Athenian cavalry at Corinth numbered 600; but the hard fighting was between the foot-soldiers, and the cavalry were scarcely engaged. Only eleven of the latter fell, and their names are recorded in two lines, six in the first, and five, including Dexileôs, in the second, on the handsome public monument referred to by Pausanias, i 29 § 8, which was found in the Cerameicus, and is now in the Central Museum.[2] But while the historians are silent on the prowess of the 'five horsemen,' it is just possible that we may be able to find an incidental illustration of this unrecorded exploit in the pages of the Greek orators. In a speech written by Lysias, the youthful and high-spirited knight, Mantitheus, states that at the battle of Corinth he fought in

[1] *Essays on Art and Archæology*, p. 199.
[2] E. L. Hicks, *Greek Historical Inscriptions*, No. 68.

the front rank, and that in the engagement his own tribe had suffered more severely than any other.¹ Can we establish any connexion between this 'tribe' and Dexileôs of Thoricus? I think we can. The name of the tribe to which Mantitheus belonged is not recorded in the speech itself; but we may fairly regard Mantitheus as a member of the same family as the person known to us, from the first speech of Demosthenes against Bœotus, as 'Mantias the son of Mantitheus of the *deme* of Thoricus.' It would follow from this that Thoricus was also the *deme* of the Mantitheus who fought at Corinth, and, it will be observed, it is to this very *deme* that our Dexileôs belonged. Dexileôs is thus identified as a member of the tribe, the tribe *Acamantis*, which bore the brunt of the battle, and it was probably in the battle itself that he fell, possibly with the four horsemen whose names are recorded in the same line as himself in the public monument of the same engagement.

From the Street of Tombs I walked out to Colonus, and soon reached the well-known hill, crowned with the monuments of those distinguished archæologists, Otfried Müller and Charles

---

¹ Lysias, Or. xvi § 15, μάλιστα τῆς ἡμετέρας φυλῆς δυστυχησάσης καὶ πλείστων ἐνθανόντων.

Lenormant. The surroundings of the hill are not so bowery as might be expected from the language of the famous chorus in the *Œdipus Coloneus*, but its level summit commands a pleasing view of a broad belt of olive-trees extending as far as the eye can reach along both the banks of the Cephisus.

March 31.—The bird's-eye view of Marathon from the summit of Pentelicus had been so perfect, that we gave up our original intention of driving to the battlefield itself, thus gaining a day for a delightful excursion to another spot of historic interest, the ancient fort of Phyle. The fort is about thirteen miles north-west of Athens, and occupies a commanding position in the range of Parnes, towards the Bœotian frontier. At a quarter to nine we started in an open carriage for Chassia, a village lying a few miles west of the site of Acharnæ. After we had got out into the country, the road became singularly bad, being in many parts nothing but the dry bed of a torrent. Fortunately, we had the same driver as on our excursion to Pentelicus, and we had frequent occasion to admire his skill in driving over apparently impassable places, where the winter rains had washed away the soil, and had laid bare the broken masses of rock. As we approached

Chassia the rugged range of Parnes increased in grandeur, till we were in full view of the lofty ridge of Harma, ending to the right in a bold precipice.

In two hours and a quarter we reached the village and drew up at the first house, where a local official introduced to us a tall man in a blue jacket and a red cap, who was to guide us to the ruined fort. After going through the little village, we met a number of peasants laden with wood which they had cut on the hillsides to burn into charcoal, as the men of the neighbouring village of Acharnæ used to do long ago. A delightful walk through the woods and along the upland streams brought us in about an hour to a very small monastery, consisting of a diminutive chapel with a few rooms and stables, set on the verge of a ravine, and called, from its surroundings, the monastery of the Παναγία τῶν κλειστῶν (Our Lady of the Glen). Here we waited for half an hour, while one of the monks, who had ridden up on his pony just before us, entertained us with coffee and bread and honey. After a steep walk for another hour, we reached the fort.

The remains were far more perfect than I had expected. On the western side it is protected by steep precipices; on the eastern, it can only be entered by a gradual ascent from the north, so contrived that the enemy could not approach without exposing his unprotected right to the missiles of the holders of the fortress. The walls are built of large blocks of squared stone, and are in excellent preservation on the north and east. Enclosed within these walls, and almost on a level with them, is a grass-grown platform, consisting of an irregular quadrilateral, only 300 yards in circumference. From this summit, which is 2090 feet above the sea, the view to the north is closed by part of the loftier range of Parnes, rising beyond the upland pastures, across which lies the path into Bœotia, commanded by the fort. To the south, you look down on the rugged cliffs of a magnificent ravine; and beyond this, framed in a prospect which embraces the Saronic Gulf and the mountains of Epidaurus, you descry, in the middle distance, the hill of Lycabettus and the rock of the Acropolis. It lends a new interest to the historic associations of the spot when we find that the patriotic band of exiles who, in the month of January B.C. 403, rallied round Thrasybulus, held the fort against the Three Thousand, and, with their numbers increased from seventy to seven hundred, defeated the adherents of the Thirty in their camp between Phyle and Acharnæ, marched to the Peiræus, fought the battle of Munychia, and restored the constitution, must again and again have looked from this lofty fortress toward the citadel of Athens, and derived fresh courage from seeing before them the goal of their hopes.

We found the star of Bethlehem and other flowers growing on the grassy platform, and also, in still greater profusion, by the wayside, as we returned by a somewhat more direct route, down a rough path into Chassia. Near the village we noticed several picturesque groups of women and children with dark, handsome faces, and with flowing draperies of bright colours. We drove back by a much better road than the one by which we had come in the morning, passed through avenues of olive-trees, crossed the Cephisus, and soon afterwards entered Athens.

April 1.—I called on the manager of the Ionian Bank, who kindly gave me a letter of introduction to M. Serpieri, the well-known director of the French mining company at Laurium. We then went to the bazaar, where I bought a tobacco-pouch of red leather to serve as a purse for the heaps of coppers that one has to carry about with one in a country where copper and paper form the usual currency, and where gold and silver are seldom seen. After this we spent several hours on a third visit to the Acropolis, where I went carefully over many of the details of the Parthenon, the Erechtheum, and the Propylæa, and was glad to identify in the distance the crag of Phyle, which we had climbed on the previous day.

The rugged platform of the Acropolis was thickly strewn with countless flowers looking like large daisies. It was possibly some such flower as this that suggested the tasteful lines 'on a daisy from the Parthenon':—

> 'This very one looked from the Parthenon;
>   O simple flower! what splendid fate was thine!
> Now the Greek glory is about thee thrown,
>   And oldest archives seem thy leaves to line.
>
> For me hereafter shall the daisies hold
>   Hints of the Virgin's Temple in their face;
> Of fabled Phidian wonders, white and gold,
>   Shall Fancy mind me in each common place.'[1]

But the flower that I saw, as I afterwards ascertained, was not a variety of daisy, but was really the *anthemis Chia*, which is frequent in the south of Europe, and is extremely common in Attica, where it flowers from the latter part of January to the latter part of August.[2]

[1] Charlotte Fiske Bates, in *Poems of Places*, Greece, p. 63.
[2] Heldreich's *Pflanzen der Attischen Ebene*, 1877, pp 500, 567,

At 3.30 we left for Laurium by the new railway, stopping on our way at several very unpretentious stations. Over one of these, which was only a small shed, I saw the name of *Liopesi*, a village on the site of Pæania, the *deme* of Demosthenes. It lies at the foot of the north-eastern

in A. Mommsen's *Griechische Jahreszeiten*, v. Sibthorp's *Flora Græca*, fig. 884.

One of the most interesting questions as to the Flora of the Acropolis is that raised by Plutarch's statement, that, during Sulla's siege of Athens, the distressed Athenians fed on a plant which he describes as τὸ παρθένιον τὸ περὶ τὴν ἀκρόπολιν φυόμενον (*Sulla*, 13 § 2). Dr. Holden identifies this as the 'fever-few, a plant of the chamomile kind' [*matricaria parthenium*], and quotes Pliny's story of a favourite slave of Pericles who fell from the top of the Parthenon and was healed of his bruises by means of a plant which obtained the name of *parthenium* from its virtues being revealed in a dream by the virgin goddess herself. (The 'slave' was Mnesicles, the architect of the Propylæa.) I may add that the Greek chamomile begins to flower in the latter half of January, and has a more agreeable smell and a pleasanter taste than other kinds (Heldreich, p. 567). Dr. Holden's reviewer in the *Academy* for 11th Dec. 1886, p. 392, appears to assume that it was the *flowers* of the παρθένιον that were eaten, and adds that the *chrysanthemum coronarium*, 'and nothing else of the kind, was flowering on the Akropolis in March 1883.' But the *chrysanthemum coronarium* does not flower until after the beginning of March, and it was on the first of March that Athens was taken by Sulla. The reviewer's inquiry whether it 'could ever be made edible' is, however, answered by its being mentioned by Heldreich among the plants whose tender shoots are used as vegetables in Attica during the winter and spring. It resembles the *anthemis Chia*, but its outer flowers are yellow instead of white (Sibthorp, fig. 877).

end of the range of Hymettus, where the mountain terminates in a rugged and precipitous cliff. While our train moved slowly on, we had fine views of Pentelicus, and afterwards of the wild country in the south-east of Attica.

The name of Laurium, which in ancient times was applied to the mining district in general, is now given to the modern mining village, which also bears the name of *Ergasteria*. The modern Laurium, at which we arrived after six o'clock, is a dreary little place, with a number of small houses on the four sides of an open space of bare and dusty ground. After finding our inn, the *Hôtel de l'Europe* (where some very unpalatable tea was served us in two tumblers of thick glass), we called at about seven o'clock on M. Serpieri, who gave us a most kind and cordial reception. He would gladly have put us up for the night, had we not already taken a room at the wretched little inn— a dirty place, where it proved almost impossible to sleep. He at once arranged for his brother-in-law and partner, M. Ernest Pellissier, to meet us early the next morning, and drive us first to Sunium and afterwards to the mines.

April 2.—At half-past seven in the morning, we started for Sunium in an open carriage drawn by three horses, in company with M. Pellissier, who, as we soon found, had spent some time at Newcastle, and was very fairly familiar with English. Even the road to Sunium had been constructed by the French company, who are very public-spirited people and apparently do a great deal that in other countries would be done at the public expense. The wild flowers by the roadside, and the bright little bays of blue water which we passed on our left, added much to our enjoyment. After a rapid drive of about an hour, followed by a short walk, we reached the famous ruins of the temple of Athene with its radiant columns, not mellowed with hues of amber like those of the Parthenon, but standing in stainless glory in a magnificent situation on the breezy height at the end of the headland: 'Tritonia's airy shrine,' that 'gleams along the wave.' The most conspicuous part of the ruins is the row of nine lofty columns that give to the cape its mediæval and modern name of Cape Colonna. 'On Sunium's marbled steep' we lingered for a while, looking across the Ægean to the southern promontories of Eubœa, and to Andros and Tenos, and all

'Those blessed isles
Which, seen from far Colonna's height,
Make glad the heart that hails the sight.'

It was not without some regret at the unavoidable shortness of our stay that we hastened back to the carriage and returned to Laurium, which we entered before ten. After being hospitably entertained by M. Serpieri, we started off again with M. Pellissier at half-past eleven and drove inland towards the works of the French company, through some wild and rugged scenery, with rough hillsides partly covered with low brushwood. On our way, we passed through the small village formed by the company for their work-people, with the two churches which they had also built, on two opposite heights, one for those of the Greek, the other for those of the Roman communion. After about an hour's drive we reached the mines, which are connected with Laurium by special lines of railway. As I wanted to see something of the works themselves, I was introduced to the chief engineer, a particularly pleasant young fellow, who made me put on a blouse and a small leather helmet in preparation for the descent. I went in his company down one of the shafts, the one that was named after M. Serpieri himself, and, on alighting, traversed several of the long galleries, where I was shown the far narrower and less regular passages worked by the miners in ancient times. These passages,

I was told, were found to be frequently of a spiral form, and sometimes hardly left room enough for a man to crawl through. Old tools and water-jugs and niches for lamps have occasionally been found, but I saw none of these myself. A 'small museum' of these finds is mentioned in Baedeker's excellent guide-book, but I could discover nothing about it on the spot; on my return to Cambridge, however, I learnt from Professor Middleton that its contents had gone to the Louvre. It is sometimes supposed that the modern miners confine themselves to extracting, by means of improved processes, the large amount of lead ore and the very small quantity of silver that still remain in the ancient refuse. This is not the case, at any rate with the French company, who have extensive mines, excavated by themselves, which it would take, I was told, several days to traverse. They export their lead mainly to Newcastle, and their zinc to Swansea and Antwerp. On leaving the works we were presented with a large number of beautiful specimens of galena, aragonite, and other minerals; and after a most interesting visit, were driven back to our inn, where we had more than an hour to spare before the 3.35 train which brought us back to Athens at 6.10, much delighted with the kind and hospitable reception we had met with on this our last excursion in Attica. It was a day that, for myself, had added a fresh interest to the dry details of the Attic law of mines, as contained in the *Pantænctus* of Demosthenes ; while it had also given a new significance to the prayer of the chorus of Salaminian sailors in the *Ajax* of Sophocles (1217-1222) :—

> γενοίμαν ἵν' ὑλᾶεν ἔπεστι πόντου
> πρόβλημ' ἁλίκλυστον, ἄκραν
> ὑπὸ πλάκα Σουνίου,
> τὰς ἱερὰς ὅπως
> προσείποιμεν Ἀθάνας.

> Waft me where yon wooded steep,
> Washed by waves, hangs o'er the deep,
> Under Sunium's level crest ;
> So may we
> Shout *Hail!* to thee,
> And thy temples, Athens blest.

III

ATHENS TO NAUPLIA—TIRYNS—ARGOS—MYCENÆ—NEMEA—CORINTH

οἳ δ' Ἄργος τ' εἶχον Τίρυνθά τε τειχιόεσσαν . . .
οἳ δὲ Μυκήνας εἶχον ἐϋκτίμενον πτολίεθρον,
ἀφνειόν τε Κόρινθον.   ILIAD, ii 559, 569.

APRIL 3.—We rose early and drove down to the Peiræus in time for the steamer of the Hellenic Company which starts at seven for Nauplia. Our steamer was the *Elpis*, one of the best boats of the best of the three Greek companies. There were a goodly number of Greeks on board, many of them country folk, one of whom arrested my attention by loud and repeated calls for Sophocles, who, however, did not respond. From first to last the voyage was most delightful. As we steamed out of port we had a fine retrospect of the hills that stand around the Acropolis; and, while approaching the island of Ægina, we enjoyed a distant view of the ruined columns of its famous temple. After seeing several smaller islands, we passed under the wild and rugged cliffs of Methana, a peninsula rising to the height of 2431 feet, and thus attaining an elevation about 700 feet above the highest point in Ægina. The volcanic origin of this peninsula is the subject of an elaborate description in the *Metamorphoses* of Ovid (xv 296-306), and the date of its upheaval is ascribed by Pausanias (ii 34 § 2) to the time of Antigonus, who died in 239 B.C.

Steaming onwards to the south-east between Methana and Ægina, we passed close under the island of Poros, with its hilly slopes clothed with groves of citron, an island which once bore the name of Calaureia, and was the scene of the death of Demosthenes. It was here that he sought sanctuary from the emissaries of Antipater in the temple of Poseidon. In the second of the letters that bear his name, a letter whose genuineness has, in recent years, found an able champion in Professor Blass, who sees in it nothing unworthy of Demosthenes, in point of either thought or language, we find the orator writing from exile to his countrymen:—'I have seated myself in the sanctuary of Poseidon in Calaureia, not only because of the protection which I hope the god will afford me, . . . but also because from that island I can on every day look across to my country.' Thus we may picture to ourselves the exiled orator spending some of his latest hours in full view of the Athens which he had loved and served with a patriot's devotion. It occurs to us to inquire whether there is anything to prevent the traveller from seeing the same view from the same spot at the present day, and the inquiry is forced upon us by a remarkable statement in Stanley's brilliant essay on Greek Topography in the first volume of the *Classical Museum*, 1844, p. 78 :— 'The view of Athens which Demosthenes enjoyed from the island of Calaurea, has since been intercepted by the volcanic irruption of the ridge of Methana.' Similarly, Mr. Tozer, in his admirable lectures on the geography of Greece, refers to this passage with the remark that 'had this mountain existed in the time of Demosthenes, it would have prevented him from enjoying a view of Athens from the island Calaureia, for it directly intervenes between those two points' (p. 137). Lastly, from Mr. Tozer's lectures the remark has been transferred to the pages of Murray's *Greece*, 1884, ii 460, where it is argued that, as Athens cannot now be seen from Calaureia, the promontory of Methana must have been formed since the death of Demosthenes. The conclusion is possibly correct, but the reason assigned is certainly wrong. It is only necessary to turn to a good map to find that, looking from Calaureia, we should see the promontory of Methana in the direction of Corinth and not in that of Athens; and also that a straight line drawn from Calaureia to Athens clears the eastern coast of Ægina, and passes far to the east of Methana. Lastly, it appears from an observation in Curtius's *Peloponnesos*, ii 449, that, if one stands near the site of the sanctuary of Poseidon, at the head of a ravine down which a little stream descends to the sea, one can still see the Acropolis to the right of Ægina, as in the days of Demosthenes.

After leaving the bay of Poros, which, from 1830 to 1877 was the naval arsenal of Greece, we rounded the easternmost point of Argolis, and soon after passed between the rocky shores of the mainland and the long and rugged island of Hydra, famous for the part played by its bold sailors in the Greek war of independence. We touched at the capital, which bears the same name as the island, and presents a very striking aspect with its bright houses piled up the sides of the steep hills which form a kind of amphitheatre above the harbour. Almost equally interesting was the island of Spezzia, on leaving which the steamer entered the Argolic Gulf, and brought us into full view of some of the lofty mountains of the east coast of Laconia. During the day, while turning round the bold promontories of Argolis, we had repeated opportunities of viewing from various directions, from the north, the east, and the south, the twin tops of Mount Didymi, rising to the height of more than 3500 feet above the sea.

We reached Nauplia about six o'clock and went to the *Hôtel Mycenæ* with a French lady and gentleman, who had been agreeable fellow-passengers during the day's voyage, and also with an accomplished German professor from Berlin. The Frenchman, the German, and ourselves soon started off together to ascend the fort of Palamidi, which is 700 feet above the sea and is approached by a flight of 715 steep steps. We had to wait some little time before our small party of representatives of three separate nations obtained formal permission to visit the fort. We were escorted by a young Greek soldier who had apparently but lately arrived in Nauplia, as he had soon to stop to ask another soldier the way up the steps. From the balcony of one of the upper rooms we enjoyed an extensive view of the Laconian mountains glowing in the sunset. Instead of descending the long flight of steps, we returned by a needlessly circuitous route over extremely rough stones which brought us back to our hotel after dark.

April 4.—In the morning we walked along the high-road towards Argos as far as Tiryns, which is about an hour's walk from Nauplia. On arriving at the ruins, which lie on some rising ground immediately to the right of the road, we went through one of the great galleries, built of enormous blocks of stone, and thus reached the site of the 'Royal Residence,' recently excavated by Schliemann. The ground-plan of the principal approach to the palace, of the great gateway, and of some of the rooms, may be readily traced. Among the apartments that are most easily identified is the bath-room with a large slab of bluish stone for its floor, and a channel of white stone to carry off the water. But the massive walls and the enormous galleries were far more interesting than any of these minor details; and one of the most enjoyable sights afforded by our visit to the ruins was the view of the lofty fort of Palamidi and the bold headland of Nauplia.

As we passed a clump of reeds on our return, we heard a noise resembling that of a number of paroquets quarrelling. It was only the Greek frogs, who continue to croak in much the same manner as that described in the *Frgos* of Aristophanes. But the noise that I heard would be more accurately represented by *kcke-kekék kodk kodk* than by the *brekekekéx kodx kodx* of the comic poet. I failed to catch either the initial *br* or the final *s*.[1] Nauplia itself presented an animated appearance as we re-entered it. It was market-day, and the costumes of the men, who had come in from the country in their great cloaks of white wool, gave a singularly oriental effect to the scene.

During the afternoon we sat out of doors, on an unfrequented path below the fort of Palamidi, with the Laconian mountains in full view across the water, and with the waves rippling at some little distance below our feet. Our seclusion was suddenly interrupted by a large stone bounding down the hillside from the fort of Palamidi. Fortunately, we observed its approach before it reached us, and we watched it dashing down toward the waves close to the spot where we were sitting.

We have our meals, not in the hotel itself, but in a neighbouring restaurant under the same management. At seven in the evening the scene

[1] Dodwell's *Tour*, ii 45; Mure's *Tour*, ii 262; and Clark's *Peloponnesus*, p. 103. The Greek frog is the *rana esculenta*.

was remarkably animated. Among the guests were a large number of soldiers, who gave constant employment to the solitary boy who was waiting on all of us, and was rushing about the room answering every call with shouts of ἔφθασε—the modern Greek for *anon, anon, sir.*

April 5.—Our excursion for to-day was a drive to Argos and Mycenæ. Before sunrise I was awakened by the songs of the birds, and recalled the opening scene of the *Electra* of Sophocles, where, on the morning of the return of Orestes to Mycenæ, the aged attendant says to Orestes and Pylades:—

ὡς ἡμὶν ἤδη λαμπρὸν ἡλίου σέλας
ἑῷα κινεῖ φθέγματ' ὀρνίθων σαφῆ,
μέλαινά τ' ἄστρων ἐκλέλοιπεν εὐφρόνη.

For lo! at length the radiant light of day
Wakes to our ears the morning-song of birds,
And the dark night of stars has passed away.

After an early breakfast on oranges and bread and honey, we started at half-past seven, and drove past Tiryns, and then along a rather rough road, straight across the plain of Argos. In little more than an hour we reached Argos itself, which consists of a large number of mean houses closely packed together. We stopped first at the museum, a single room on the ground floor of the *Demarchia*, in the same building as the local school. The schoolmaster unlocked the door and threw back the shutters for us, to the delight of a number of inquisitive boys who followed us round the room. Here we saw numerous fragments of sculpture, mainly from the *Heræum*. There was also a relief representing a youth holding a spear and standing beside his horse in an attitude suggested by the famous *doryphoros* of the Argive sculptor Polycleitus;[1] and a statuette of a nymph planting her foot on a prostrate swan, in a pose somewhat resembling that of the Venus de Milo. Besides these there were several inscriptions and marble heads and bits of honeysuckle pattern from the *Heræum*.

We here inquired for some one to show us the way to the theatre and to the summit of Larissa, the acropolis of Argos. The usher, a dull creature, presented himself for this purpose, though we would gladly have secured one of his bright pupils instead. However, several of the boys joined us and made themselves useful in showing the way to our 'guide.' We soon reached the theatre, which is here, as often elsewhere, hewn in the solid rock out of the side of the hill. It is on the south-

[1] South Kensington Gallery of Antique Casts, No. 72.

west side of the acropolis, and commands from its upper rows of seats a magnificent view of Nauplia and the neighbouring hills. Had not the loneliness of the scene been broken by the presence of the group of boys, one might have found it easier to picture to oneself the 'not ignoble citizen of Argos,' who, according to Horace, was wont to pass his time listening to imaginary plays in the solitude of this theatre—

> 'qui se credebat miros audire tragœdos
> in vacuo lætus sessor plausorque theatro.'
>
> *Ep.* ii 2, 129.

A few steps beyond the theatre our attention was directed to an ancient relief representing a warrior with a round Argive shield, on a rearing horse, with a serpent erect before it. The horse was doubtless meant as an emblem of Argos, Ἄργεος ἱπποβότοιο (*Odyss.* iii 263). The shield, and possibly even the serpent, refers to the ancient name of Aspis, by which the castle of Argos was designated, according to the testimony of Plutarch.[1]

From this point we were taken straight up the hill by a steep and stony ascent, under a burning sun, with no trace of a path until we had accom-

---

[1] Pyrrh. 32, Ἀσπὶς ὀχυρὰ καὶ δυσκαθαίρετος. Cleom. 17, ὁ περὶ τὴν Ἀσπίδα τόπος ὑπὲρ τοῦ θεάτρου χαλεπὸς καὶ δυσπρόσοδος.— Curtius, *Peloponnesos*, ii 354.

plished about two-thirds of our climb. Near the summit we refreshed ourselves with draughts of deliciously cold water from one of the cisterns which have been used for many ages by the successive holders of the acropolis. The ruins on the summit are of Byzantine and Frank origin, and the outworks of the fort cover a considerable space of ground. Through one of the arches of the ruined walls we had a lovely view of part of the surrounding country; while from the summit itself, which is nearly 1000 feet above the sea, about 300 feet higher than Palamidi, we had an extensive prospect, including Mount Artemisium to the west, and Mount Arachnæum to the east, with Mount Eubœa to the north-east rising above the site of Mycenæ.

After descending rapidly to the foot of the hill, we drove on, at about eleven o'clock, towards Mycenæ. Outside of Argos we left the main road for one that was still worse, and our horses had soon to cross the rushing torrent of the ancient *Charadros*, at a point where the bridge had been swept away. It was here that the Argive armies of old were wont to settle any disputes that had arisen during the campaign, before they re-entered the walls of the town; and it was doubtless with the stones from the dry bed of this torrent that, on an occasion mentioned by Thucydides, they began to stone their general Thrasyllus for negotiating a truce with the Spartan king, Agis.[1] Shortly after this we crossed the *Inachos* itself, by a bridge that was fast falling into ruins. To the east of our road we caught a glimpse of the site of the famous *Heræum*, standing on the spot associated with the story of Cleobis and Biton, and with the incident of the conflagration of the temple caused by the carelessness of the aged priestess Chrysis (Thuc. iv 133). The site was long unknown, and even Leake failed to find it. It was accidentally discovered by Mr. Finlay and Mr. Gordon while they were out shooting one day in 1833. All that we could see, with the help of a glass, was a ruinous heap of stones in the middle of a green terrace, and three bars of remains corresponding presumably to the three successive platforms of the temple precincts.

About noon we reached the village of Kharvati, and were at once met by the custodian of the ruins of Mycenæ, Petros Christópoulos, a wiry man with brown and sunburnt features, in whose company we set off on our walk of some twenty

---

[1] B.C. 418. Thuc. v 60 § 5, τόν τε Θράσυλλον ἀναχωρήσαντες ἐν τῷ Χαράδρῳ, οὗπερ τὰς ἀπὸ στρατιᾶς δίκας πρὶν εἰσιέναι κρίνουσιν ἤρξαντο λεύειν.

minutes, across the low hills to the ruins, passing on our right the remains of an ancient bridge over which the Sacred Way once passed to the *Heræum.* Our visit to the ruins began with the so-called treasure-house, or tomb, of Atreus—a huge vaulted structure with a roof resembling a bee-hive, formed of massive stones laid in horizontal lines from the floor to the top. Some of those at the top had slipped out, thus allowing the light to fall on the interior of the dome. The surface of the interior was doubtless at one time completely covered with plates of bronze; the marks of the nails used to fasten the plates are still to be seen. To the right of the central chamber there is a short passage leading out of it into a far smaller recess.

After passing a similar structure, the so-called tomb of Clytæmnestra, we walked along the hillside to the famous Gate of Lions, with its lintel formed by a huge block of stone no less than fifteen feet in length. Entering the gate, we very soon reached the tiny *agora,* a circular space, about 100 feet in diameter, surrounded by a continuous double row of upright stones, with horizontal slabs stretching across the top from one row to the other. More than half of the space within the circle was occupied by the five tombs excavated by Schliemann, which produced the extremely curious and interesting ornaments of gold, as well as the other remains we had seen at Athens.

A short climb brought us to the acropolis, where we lingered for a while on the level lawn, near the top of the hill—a lawn rich with soft herbage and bright with scarlet anemones and stars of Bethlehem. From this point you can descry, to the north-west, the summit of Cyllene, and to the south-west, the snowy ridge of Taygetus, while close at hand, on the east, rises a rugged mass of hills, the nearest of which is now called by the name of *Sāra*. But the traveller looks in vain for the Arachnæan height, on which the watchman in the *Agamemnon* sees the last of the successive beacon-fires that tell of the fall of Troy. The view of this height, now known as *Arna*, is intercepted by the nearer hills. The *Heræum* is also quite invisible from Mycenæ; it is thus as impossible, as it is unnecessary, to reconcile the local indications suggested in the opening scene of the *Electra* with the actual topography of Mycenæ and its neighbourhood.

We returned to Kharvati by a slightly different route, and spent a short time in the local museum—a small room crowded with unimportant fragments of stone and pottery. We here saw the contents of a tomb, with some remains which are fancifully called the bones of Agamemnon. After thus pleasantly spending a couple of hours at the ruins of Mycenæ, we drove back to Nauplia.

April 6.—We rose betimes, and started at half-past six on our drive to Corinth. During the earlier part of the day it was pleasantly cool, while we drove past the now familiar walls of Tiryns and the acropolis of Argos. After leaving the latter, we continued our course along the main route, instead of diverging to the right as we had done the day before. Of the ruins of Mycenæ little indeed could be seen from the road; but we were able to identify the grassy plateau of its acropolis and some few fragments of its shattered walls. So true at the present day is the Homeric description of the 'city of Mycenæ rich in gold,' lying ' in a *nook* of the horse-pasturing plain of Argos.'[1]

The scenery became wilder as we left the plain of Argos for the mountain district to the north, and it reached its highest degree of grandeur near the narrow pass of the *trētón óros*,[2] sometimes known by its Turkish name of Dervenaki.

[1] *Odyss.* iii 305, πολυχρύσοιο Μυκήνης, and 263, μύχῳ Ἄργεος ἱπποβότοιο.—Clark's *Peloponnesus*, p. 67.

[2] Diodorus, iv 11; Pausanias, ii 15 § 1, ὁδὸς ἐπὶ τοῦ καλουμένου τρητοῦ, στενὴ μὲν καὶ αὐτὴ περιεχόντων ὀρῶν, ὀχήματι δέ ἐστιν ὅμως ἐπιτηδειοτέρα.

This is the nearest point to Nemea, which lies a few miles beyond the hills to the west. We accordingly left our carriage, and secured an active boy to show us the way there. He took us over a rough track across broken ground covered with brushwood, until at last we looked down on the level valley of the 'deep-plained,' the 'well-watered' Nemea.[1] It is a fertile tract of land, almost completely encircled by high hills. The most prominent of these is Phuka, which rises in the north to the height of nearly 3000 feet. It corresponds to the ancient Apesas, where Perseus is said to have offered sacrifices to the Apesantian Zeus,[2] and is a mountain of most fantastic form, the top consisting of a level table-land with a gradual ascent to the left and a short and abrupt precipice to the right.

As we dropped into the valley, we soon caught sight of the three gray columns of the ruined temple of the Nemean Zeus. Shortly afterwards, while walking across the little plain, past fields of rising corn, we were struck by the number of wild flowers that met the eye. Among them were stars of Bethlehem, grape-hyacinths and purple

[1] Pindar, *Nem.* iii (18) 30, ἐν βαθυπέδῳ Νεμέᾳ, and Theocritus, xxv 182, εὐύδρου Νεμέης.
[2] Pausanias, ii 15 § 3; Callimachus, fragm. 82.

irises; but the brightest and most conspicuous of all was the scarlet anemone, which is one of the most characteristic flowers of the Greek springtime. Its enduring presence on Hellenic soil attests the truthfulness of Pindar's epithet for the season of spring, the epithet φοινικάνθεμον (Pyth. iv 64 = 114). It also appears to be conclusive in favour of our looking for some similar epithet in the fragment of Pindar which, according to the common text, refers to a supposed palm-tree at Nemea, where no such tree is now to be seen. The date-palm may be seen growing at Nauplia and other places on the coast, but it is in no way characteristic of spring nor is there anything exceptional in the aspect of its foliage on the approach of that season.[1]

To the left of the ruined temple stands the very recent village of Heracleia, to which the inhabitants of the neighbouring village of Kersomati have transferred themselves after having their homes laid desolate by earthquakes. The same

---

[1] Fragment 53 [45], ἐν Ἀργείᾳ Νεμέᾳ μάντιν οὐ λανθάνει φοίνικος ἔρνος [φοίνικος ἐανῶν MSS, φοινικοεάνων Koch, followed by Fennell], ὁπότ' οἰχθέντος ὡρῶν θαλάμου εὔοδμον ἐπαΐωσιν ἔαρ φυτὰ νεκτάρεα. Pausanias, however, after distinguishing the crowns awarded in the Olympic and other games, adds: οἱ δὲ ἀγῶνες φοίνικος ἔχουσιν οἱ πολλοὶ στέφανον· ἐς δὲ τὴν δεξιάν ἐστι καὶ πανταχοῦ τῷ νικῶντι ἐστιθέμενος φοῖνιξ (viii 48 § 2).

cause has led to the gradual destruction of the Nemean temple, only three of whose columns are still standing, one of the east front and two of the eastern end of the inner temple. On reaching the ruins, we found fragments of the other columns strewn about in all directions. Even in the time of Pausanias, who found the temple surrounded by a grove of cypresses, the roof had already fallen in (ii 15 § 2). While using my compass to take the bearings of the surrounding hills, I soon became the centre of an interested group of children, who had been looking on, in an unobtrusive way, while my wife was sketching the view. I explained to them the quarters of the compass (ἄρκτος, μεσημβρία, ἀνατολή and δύσις), and tried to extract from them the names of some of the hills that surrounded their home. They were very positive that the highest hill to the south-west was called *Megalovunó*. This corresponds to the Kēlūsa of Xenophon,[1] which rises 4166 feet above the sea, and is one of the 'primeval mountains' that look down on the little plain of Phlius.[2] They were, probably with less reason, equally positive that the small hill to the east was called by no name at all (τίποτε); though it is

[1] *Hellenica*, iv 7 § 7; Bursian, *Geogr.* ii 32.
[2] Pindar, *Nem.* vi 74, ἀσκίοις Φλιοῦντος ὑπ' ὠγυγίοις ὄρεσιν.

doubtless the hill which bears the name of *Korako-vuni*. High up the sides of this hill I could make out, with the help of a glass, the dark recesses which are sometimes regarded as the legendary haunt of the Nemean lion.

After staying for a while among the ruins, where, as elsewhere in this secluded valley, the anemones were in full flower, we turned aside to visit the remains of a mediæval church with fragments of the temple embedded in its walls. From this point we walked uphill toward the east, by a path to the north of that by which we had entered the valley. We thus traced the little stream that was running down the path till we found its source in a fountain near some aspens to our left. The fountain is probably the same as that known to the ancients by the name of Adrasteia (Pausanias, ii 15 § 3); and we gladly quenched our thirst, and that of our sturdy little guide, with cool draughts from the ancient spring. Meanwhile, to the right of our path, we had been passing some scanty memorials of the Nemean games. One of these is the site of the theatre, marked by a semicircular recess on the side of the hill, and, crossing this at a lower level, are the faint traces of the *stadium*. That these traces are so faint is probably due in part to the frequent earthquakes, and also to the action of the stream that runs along the middle of the course. In choosing a site for a *stadium*, one of the most obvious expedients was to select the bed of a grassy dell, which had been partly hollowed out by a stream; to divert this stream, and to level its bed. This is clearly what was done in the case of the *stadium* used for the Isthmian games, where the stream which was once diverted has since re-asserted itself, has broken through the shelving banks of the upper end of the *stadium*, and now runs down the very middle of the course.

We passed banks that were bright with purple irises, as we left the valley, by a new road joining the main route, and regained our carriage after a *détour* of not more than two hours and a half. We then drove on towards Corinth, having varied views of the mountains behind us and at some distance from us on either side, until we reached the base of the massive rock of the Acrocorinthus and gradually descended into New Corinth, where we arrived at half-past five.

The railway from Corinth to Nauplia was opened on this day; in the morning we had observed a chorus of Argive elders falling into picturesque groups, while with due deliberation they put the finishing touches to the line; during the day we had noticed the peasants driving their cattle along the level railroad instead of the rugged highway; and late in the afternoon, as we passed the foot of the Acrocorinthus, we had the satisfaction of seeing the saloon carriage that was bearing the King of the Hellenes on the first railway journey to Nauplia.

Our hotel at New Corinth was the *Hôtel de la Couronne*, a small but clean establishment belonging to the same proprietors as our hotel at Athens. In the evening we went down to the beach beyond the landing-place and sat down with the Achæan coast extending to our left, beyond the site of Sikyon; in front of us, across the calm waters of the gulf of Corinth, was the rugged foreland of the Peræa, while beyond the northern shore there rose in the light of sunset the sombre slopes of Helicon and the silver snows of Parnassus.

During the night the quiet of our hotel was somewhat seriously disturbed by a large party of patriotic Greeks, who selected its *salle à manger*, as the most suitable place in Corinth to celebrate the sixty-fifth anniversary of the outbreak of the Greek war of independence in 1821.

April 7.—After an early breakfast we started at seven o'clock to drive to Old Corinth. We began by keeping for some distance to the shore of the gulf; we then ascended by a winding road, until, after an hour's drive, we reached the small village that occupies part of the site of the ancient city. Shortly after leaving the carriage, we visited the remains of a Doric temple, whose seven surviving columns were formerly held to be the earliest existing example of Doric architecture in Greece, but the *Heræum* at Olympia belongs to an earlier date. Walking onwards to the west, we reached a small hamlet, where I purchased for about sixpence a coin of Corinth stamped with a representation of Pegasus. From near this spot we mounted by a toilsome ascent, keeping to our right the pointed rock from which the Acrocorinthus was battered by Mohammed II in 1458. It was this outlying peak alone that was visited at considerable risk by Dodwell, who, like Leake at a later time, was prevented by the Turks from ascending the acropolis itself.[1] By and by, we reached the lower gate of the citadel, crossed the rickety drawbridge, and found ourselves at last within the walls of the upper fortification. The ground within these walls is extremely uneven and is thickly strewn with fragments of former buildings, interspersed with numerous wells and cisterns which are quite unprotected, and are sufficiently deep to

[1] Dodwell, *Classical Tour*, ii 189; Leake's *Morea*, iii 257.

be dangerous to the unwary traveller. After climbing for some little way up the lower or western summit of the enormous mass of rock which constituted the citadel of ancient Corinth, we gave up the task, and made for the higher summit which rises on the eastern side to the height of 1886 feet above the sea. On attaining this elevation we enjoyed a fairly extensive view; for, although the more distant prospect was in several directions intercepted by haze and clouds, yet we could clearly see Ægina and Salamis and Hymettus and Pentelicus (the last, five-and-fifty miles distant) to the east; the snows of Cyllene to the west; those of Parnassus toward the north; and to the south the rugged mountains of Argolis, through which we had passed on the previous day.[1] Not a soul was to be seen on any part of the

---

[1] Strabo, who visited Corinth shortly after its rebuilding by the Romans, but who did not see the wells of water on the acropolis, gives the following description of the view from the summit:—
πρὸς ἄρκτον μὲν ἀφορᾶται ὅ τε Παρνασσὸς καὶ ὁ Ἑλικών, ὄρη ὑψηλὰ καὶ νιφόβολα, καὶ ὁ Κρισαῖος κόλπος ὑποπεπτωκὼς ἀμφοτέροις, περιεχόμενος ὑπὸ τῆς Φωκίδος καὶ τῆς Βοιωτίας καὶ τῆς Μεγαρίδος καὶ τῆς ἀντιπόρθμου τῇ Φωκίδι Κορινθίας καὶ Σικυωνίας · πρὸς ἑσπέραν δὲ . . . ὑπέρκειται δὲ τούτων ἁπάντων τὰ καλούμενα Ὄνεια ὄρη διατείνοντα μέχρι Βοιωτίας καὶ Κιθαιρῶνος ἀπὸ τῶν Σκειρωνίδων πετρῶν, ἀπὸ τῆς παρὰ ταύτας ὁδοῦ πρὸς τὴν Ἀττικήν.—viii 21, p. 379.

In the same chapter Strabo says of Pirene: ὑπὸ δὲ τῇ κορυφῇ τὴν Πειρήνην εἶναι συμβαίνει κρήνην, ἔκρυσιν μὲν οὐκ ἔχουσαν μεστὴν δ' ἀεὶ

acropolis, and there was no one at hand to help us to identify, among all the cisterns near the summit, the famous fountain of Pirene. The information in Murray is entirely vague; that in Baedeker directed us in vain to the 'south-east of the highest point,' and the indications given in two such leading authorities as Curtius's *Peloponnesos* (ii 525), and Bursian's *Geographie* (ii 17), are contradictory to one another, for the former puts it to the west, and the latter 'somewhat to the east' of the summit. In my perplexity I must be content, like the poet Persius, to leave the 'pale Pirene' to others. But, with this exception alone, we have every reason to be satisfied with all that we saw during the five hours which we devoted to our excursion to the top of the Acrocorinthus.

διαυγοῦς καὶ ποτίμου ὕδατος, φασὶ δὲ καὶ ἐνθένδε καὶ ἐξ ἄλλων ὑπονόμων τινῶν φλεβίων συνθλίβεσθαι τὴν πρὸς τῇ ῥίζῃ τοῦ ὄρους κρήνην ἐκρέουσαν εἰς τὴν πόλιν ὥσθ' ἱκανῶς ἀπ' αὐτῆς ὑδρεύεσθαι. It is from this passage that Dodwell (*Classical Tour*, ii 138), borrows his description of Pirene and 'its several small rills.' In Murray's *Greece*, i 151, these become 'several limpid streams,' which are further expanded into the 'rushing streams and waterfalls tumbling down the rock,' for which Professor Mahaffy searched in vain (*Rambles in Greece*, p. 345, ed. 3.)

IV

DELPHI

ἵκεο δ' ἐς Κρίσην ὑπὸ Παρνησὸν νιφόεντα,
κνημὸν πρὸς Ζέφυρον τετραμμένον, αὐτὰρ ὕπερθεν
πέτρη ἐπικρέμαται, κοίλη δ' ὑποδέδρομε βῆσσα.
Homeric Hymn to Apollo, 282.

AT one o'clock on April 7 we went on board the *Kartería*, one of the smaller steamers of the Hellenic company, and started for Itéa, the port for Delphi. The breeze soon freshened and the waves began to be rather too rough for our little steamer; so I was one of the few passengers left on deck. My map attracted the attention of one of the Greeks on board, a sturdy, good-natured sort of a man, who took great pains to point out some of the places of special interest on our route, as we passed along the northern shore of the gulf, in sight of Cithæron, Helicon, and Parnassus. He offered us a room at Itéa, and very sensibly advised us to stop at that place instead of pushing on at once for Kastri, the village that now stands on the site of Delphi. I congratulated myself on the prospect of escaping the necessity of applying on arrival to Athanasios Kaïloiannos, the keeper of what Baedeker's *Guide* describes as *einige schmutzige Zimmer;* but, just as we were going ashore, it suddenly dawned upon me that our fellow-passenger was Athanasios himself. The rooms, however, proved to be clean enough to all outward appearance, though, as the night wore on, it became only too clear that a colony of 'Corinthians' were in possession of the place. Meanwhile, during the earlier part of the evening, we sat out in a delightful little balcony, where our hostess brought us refreshing draughts of cool water and a dish of *glykó*, made of the candied peel of the bitter orange called the *nerántzi*, the ordinary sweet orange being known by the name *portokálli*. After this we had a simple repast on fish and poached eggs. The modern Greek for fish, *psári*, is interesting, by the way, as a shortened form of the ancient *opsárion;* while poached eggs are called *avgá mátia*, the latter word being short for *ommátia*, and reminding one of the name of *Ochsen-augen*, which is given to the dish in certain parts of Germany. In the vocabulary of modern Greek, it is naturally the names of the commonest articles of everyday life that often exhibit the greatest departure from ancient usage. Thus, the old words for bread and wine and water have given way to *psômí* and *krasí* and *něró* respectively. The last of these words is the living representative of an epithet which Æschylus applied to the fountain of Dirkê, and Sophocles to draughts of water from a running spring—an epithet against which the purist Phrynichus needlessly and unavailingly protested.[1] For, at the present day, not to mention its having helped to provide a name for the *aneroid* barometer, it is in universal use in Greece, as an interesting survival from the older language, claiming kinship with *Nereus*, and boasting of a pedigree extending over thousands of years.

Itéa is the landing-place, not only for Delphi, but also for Sálona, the ancient Amphissa. Hence its other name of Scala di Salona; in ancient times it was known as Chalæon.[2] According to Ulrichs, who carefully explored all this region in 1837 and 1838, the modern name is derived from a willow

[1] Æsch. Frag. 399, ναρᾶς τε Δίρκης (explained ῥευστικῆς by Photius, who adds that ἡ συνήθεια, τρέψασα τὸ α εἰς ε, λέγει νερόν); Soph. Frag. 560, πρὸς ναρὰ δὲ (?) κρηναῖα χωροῦμεν ποτά (quoted in Etymolog. Magnum, with the explanation ναρόν· τὸ ὑγρόν); Phrynichus, 29, νηρὸν ὕδωρ μηδαμῶς, ἀλλὰ πρόσφατον, ἀκραιφνές.

[2] Pliny, *H. N.* iv 3, portus Chalæon a quo vii M. pass. introrsus liberum oppidum Delphi. Thuc. iii 101, Χαλαῖοι.

(Ἰτέα), which, many years before his time, used to stand (with a plane-tree and a poplar) beside a spring some fifteen minutes walk along the shore to the south-east.[1] In the same direction, across the outlet of the Pleistus, at the modern village of Magúla, lies the site of Cirrha, the former port of Delphi. The level land extending along the shore near the site of Cirrha is almost entirely bare of trees, as it was in the time of Pausanias (x 37 § 4), all this part of the plain having been devoted to Apollo on the conquest of Cirrha at the close of the first Sacred War (B.C. 595-585). It forms a striking contrast to the Crisæan plain, which lies farther inland and is covered with olive-trees and vineyards. The latter plain is so called from the ancient Crisa, which is sometimes confounded with Cirrha, although Cirrha lies on the coast, and Crisa several miles inland. The site of the ancient Crisa is identified by Ulrichs with some ruins called *Stepháni*, near the modern village of Chrysó on the way to Delphi.

April 8.—At eight in the morning we started on our walk to Delphi. The view of Parnassus from Itéa was remarkably fine, with its snow-clad summit glistening in the sunlight, far above the two great cliffs that rise immediately over the

[1] *Reisen und Forschungen in Griechenland*, i p. 7.

site of Delphi, which itself lies hidden behind a buttress of rock separating it from Chrysó. It was a sight that might well recall the brilliant description of the sunrise at Delphi in the *Ion* of Euripides (82-88)—

> ἅρματα μὲν τάδε λαμπρὰ τεθρίππων
> ἥλιος ἤδη κάμπτει κατὰ γῆν,
> ἄστρα δὲ φεύγει πῦρ τόδ' ἀπ' αἰθέρος
> εἰς νύχθ' ἱεράν,
> Παρνησιάδες δ' ἄβατοι κορυφαὶ
> καταλαμπόμεναι τὴν ἡμερίαν
> ἁψῖδα βροτοῖσι δέχονται.

> Lo! at last the Sun-god turneth
>   Toward the earth his chariot bright,
> And the flame in heaven that burneth
>   Drives the stars to solemn night.
> Lo! the untrodden mountain-height
>   First reflects the morning's ray,
> And Parnassus, bathed in light,
>   Greets for man the car of day.

We walked for a short distance along the highroad to Sálona, and before long met, to our surprise, a train of camels. These animals were introduced long ago by the Turks, and it is said that this is the only part of Greece where they still survive. They are certainly far more quaint and picturesque than the ordinary mules and asses that one constantly meets here and elsewhere.[1]

On reaching a prominent rock on the left of the road, we abandoned the main route, and struck off to the right, along a path that soon entered a large plantation of fine olive-trees extending over the old Crisæan plain. The waters of the Pleistus are turned in all directions into narrow channels for the purpose of irrigating these plantations. After walking for about an hour through this delightful plain with bright anemones on every side, we began to ascend the steep hill, and after a while had a beautiful retrospect of the surroundings of Itéa; the little gulf of Galaxídi, at the head of which it stands, the blue waters of the gulf of Corinth, and beyond these, the snow-clad mountains of Arcadia. By this time the day had become exceedingly hot, and, after nearly half an hour's climb, we were glad to reach the village of Chrysó with its fountains of cool water and its welcome store of oranges, with

[1] According to Mure's *Tour*, i 182, these camels 'originally formed, it is said, part of the baggage train of some of the great Turkish armaments, more especially of that fitted out against the Morea in 1822, and destroyed by the Greeks in the defiles between Argos and Corinth, upon which occasion the animals were captured and sold, and have since been employed for commercial purposes.'

which we refreshed ourselves while sitting in a balcony over a garden with a magnificent view towards the gulf. Chrysó is in point of time about half-way to Delphi.

On starting afresh, we went on by winding paths of indescribable roughness, toiling up the steep ascent, but gladdened from time to time by glorious views of the valley of Sálona, and by the cool breezes blowing toward us from the north-west over lofty mountains crowned with snow. The highest of these is now called Kiona,[1] doubtless a corruption of χιόνα, but its ancient name is quite unknown, although, excepting Olympus, it must have been the highest mountain in Greece, being no less than 8242 feet above the sea, or 174 feet higher than Parnassus itself. The view to the east was also gradually unfolding itself with its wild hillsides clothed with varied colours as bright as those of heather. At last, after an exceedingly hot and somewhat wearisome climb, we gained the crest of the hill where the great gorge of Delphi in all its height and depth bursts suddenly on the view. To the south rose the bare slopes of Kirphis, and along their base, far far below, was flowing the stream of the

---

[1] So spelt by Ross and by Vischer, *Erinnerungen*, p. 619 note; the French map has *Guiona;* Ulrichs, Γιῶνα.

Pleistus.[1] The depth of this valley far exceeded anything I had expected from the various descriptions I had read. To the north were the gleaming cliffs of the Phædriades, parted in twain by a narrow cleft. But the actual summit of Parnassus, with the snow-crowned heights that are so fine a sight in the distance, is here intercepted by the double cliff. The surrounding scenery has, of course, been the theme of many allusions in the Greek and Latin poets;[2] but the earliest description of it, in the Homeric Hymn to Apollo, still perhaps remains the best:—

Then didst thou fare unto Crisa, beneath the snowy
    Parnassus,
Crisa with shoulder of rock to the west-wind turned; but
    above it
Hangeth a cliff, and a rugged ravine ever runneth below it.

Above us, at the foot of the western cliff, far above the valley, and no less than 2300 feet above the

[1] Strabo, ix 3, πρόκειται δὲ τῆς πόλεως ἡ Κίρφις ἐκ τοῦ νοτίου μέρους, ὄρος ἀπότομον, νάπην ἀπολιπὸν μεταξύ, δι' ἧς Πλεῖστος διαρρεῖ ποταμός.

[2] Sophocles, *Antig.* 1126, ὑπὲρ διλόφου πέτρας κ.τ.λ.; Euripides, *Phœn.* 226, ὦ λάμπουσα πέτρα πυρὸς δικόρυφον σέλας ὑπὲρ ἄκρων Βακχείων; *Bacch.* 307, δικόρυφον πλάκα. [The Latin poets and some later Greek writers confound the double cliff with the actual summit of Parnassus, giving the latter the epithet *biceps* (Persius, *init.*; cf. Ovid, *Met.* i 316; Lucan. v 71; Nonnus, *Dionys.* xiii 131, Παρνησσὸν δικάρηνον).

sea, lay the mud huts of the wretched village of Kastri, which cover the site of most of the ancient buildings of Delphi. From these huts the hillside slopes downwards in successive terraces of rough and broken ground, rudely resembling the successive tiers of seats in an ancient theatre, and thus completely justifying the epithet θεατροειδὲς which Strabo applies to the site.[1] The same idea is thus expressed in Lord Houghton's stanza :—

> 'Still could I dimly trace the terraced lines
> Diverging from the cliffs on either side ;
> A theatre whose steps were filled with shrines
> And rich devices of Hellenic pride.'

In view of the great amphitheatre of hills we rested for a time, in vain endeavouring in the recesses of the rocks to find shelter from the blazing sun. It was no wonder that such a burning spot should have been selected as the central shrine for the worship of the sun-god ; and the almost complete absence of shade made one vividly conscious what a thing of naught was the 'shadow in Delphi' to which Demosthenes, at the close of his speech on the Peace, compares the utterly insignificant question on which the hotspurs of

---

[1] ix 3, p. 418, πετρῶδες χωρίον θεατροειδές, κατὰ κορυφὴν ἔχον τὸ μαντεῖον καὶ τὴν πόλιν.

Athens would have driven her to war with Philip and all his adherents in the Amphictyonic council.[1] The place where the council used to meet lay in a suburb to the right of the spot where we were resting, and, unlike Delphi itself, commanded a view of the plain through which we had come.[2] It was there, and not at Delphi, that Æschines delivered the animated but mischievous harangue reported by himself in his speech against Ctesiphon.

It occurred to me to make mention of the impiety of the people of Amphissa with regard to the consecrated land, and, from the very spot where I stood, I pointed it out to the Amphictyonic assembly; for the Cirrhæan plain lies beneath the temple and can all be seen at a single glance. 'You see,' said I, 'ye Amphictyons, how this plain has been tilled by the men of Amphissa; you see the tile-kilns they

---

[1] Autumn. B.C. 346. οὐκοῦν εὐηθὲς καὶ κομιδῇ σχέτλιον, πρὸς ἑκάστους καθ' ἕνα οὕτω προσενηνεγμένους περὶ τῶν οἰκείων καὶ ἀναγκαιοτάτων, πρὸς πάντας περὶ τῆς ἐν Δελφοῖς σκιᾶς νυνὶ πολεμῆσαι. Harpocration: Δίδυμός φησι τὴν περὶ ὄνου σκιᾶς παροιμίαν παραπεποιῆσθαι ὑπὸ τοῦ ῥήτορος κ.τ.λ. Cf. esp. Aristophanes, fragm. 238, περὶ τοῦ γὰρ ὑμῖν ὁ πόλεμος νῦν ἐστι; περὶ ὄνου σκιᾶς, and *Vesp.* 191. Macarius, *proverb. cent.* vii 8, vi 37; Zenobius, vi 28.

[2] Plutarch, *de Pyth. Or.* 29, describes the Pylæa as a kind of offshoot of Delphi: τοῖς Δελφοῖς ἡ Πυλαία συνηβᾷ καὶ συναναβόσκεται. Ulrichs, *l.c.* p. 114; and Vischer's *Erinnerungun*, p. 606 f. Curtius, in his *History of Greece*, v 411 of Ward's translation, speaks of 'the rocky terraces where the Amphictyons held their diet under the open sky.' Mahaffy's *Rambles and Studies in Greece*, chap. x p. 253-5, ed. 3.

have built there, and the stalls for their cattle. With your very eyes you can see that that accursed and devoted harbour has been furnished with fortifications. You know for yourselves, without any need of others as witnesses, that they have exacted tolls, and are levying sums of money from that consecrated harbour . . .' Late in the day the herald arose and proclaimed that all the Delphians who were of age, whether bond or free, should assemble at sunrise, with shovels and mattocks, at the spot that is there called 'the place of sacrifice'; and the same herald proclaimed further, that the Sacred Envoys and their Recorders should meet at the said spot to uphold the claims of the god and of the consecrated land. On the next day, early in the morning, we assembled at the place appointed, and went down into the Cirrhæan plain and demolished the harbour and set fire to the houses, and then returned. But, while we were so doing, the Locrians of Amphissa, who are settled at a distance of sixty furlongs from Delphi, assembled in arms, and fell upon us with their whole force, and, had we not fled to Delphi, we should have been in danger of being utterly annihilated. At the assembly of the Amphictyons, held on the next day, many further accusations were urged against the men of Amphissa, while, on the other hand, there was much praise bestowed upon our city. But the whole debate was closed by a resolution that the Sacred Envoys should, before the next ordinary assembly, appear at an appointed date at Thermopylæ, with a decree prepared for inflicting penalties on the men of Amphissa for the wrongs they had committed against the god and the consecrated land, and against the Amphictyonic council.[1]

---

[1] Æschines, *contra Ctesiphontem*, §§ 118-124, March B.C. 339.

We were proceeding uphill to the site of the ancient *stadium*, when from a ledge of rock to the left we heard a voice which proved to be that of the custodian of the antiquities of Delphi—a sturdy little man, who took us up to the *stadium*, which lies high above most of the modern buildings, and is the most loftily situated of all the ancient remains. It must have been the scene of many of the contests comprised in the Pythian games, and chiefly of the foot race, for the chariot races were held in the plain below.[1] Its shape is clearly marked out, and a few of the stone seats were still to be seen. Its total length is 630 feet, or nearly the same as that of the other *stadia* of Greece.[2]

From the *stadium* we descended towards a projecting spur of the western cliff to the fountain of *Delphusa*, near to which we refreshed ourselves with cool draughts from a tiny rill dropping from the rifted rock. The washerwomen of Kastri were in full possession of the fountain itself, which appears, indeed, to have been the public fountain of the inhabitants of Delphi in ancient times. They had also appropriated the neighbouring fountain of *Kassótis*, the waters of which descended

---

[1] Pausanias, x 37 § 4, καταβάντι δὲ ἐς τὸ πεδίον ἱππόδρομός τε ἐστι καὶ ἀγῶνα Πύθια ἄγουσιν ἐνταῦθα τὸν ἱππικόν.

[2] Leake, *Northern Greece*, ii p. 577.

into the temple of Apollo and were used for sacred purposes alone.

The guide then took us to his own cottage, where he showed us some fragments of sculpture, and brought us tumblers of cold water and 'Turkish delight,' while we sat down before a window enjoying a fine prospect of the southern hills (the range of Kirphis) and turning over the pages of the visitors' book, where we found the names of several of our friends. For some years back apparently only one lady had visited the place. We found we were the first visitors from England for the present year, the only others who had inscribed their names being a Greek from Patras and some travellers from the United States.

We resumed our rambles along the steep and dirty little paths of Kastri, between miserable little houses sorely needing the intervention of some sanitary inspector, as the modern representative of the 'purifying Apollo,' the $ἰατρόμαντις, δωμάτων καθάρσιος$.[1] We soon reached the site of the ancient theatre, but of this we only saw part of a wall, though, immediately afterwards, we were shown some fragments belonging to it, together with a few inscriptions in the neighbouring church.

Shortly after, we came across the northern wall

[1] Æschylus, *Eum.* 62, 63.

the sacred enclosure of the temple of Apollo. Near to this we saw the 'pillar of the Naxians,' bearing an inscription reserving to that people the privilege of priority in consulting the oracle, instead of having to await the result of the drawing of lots, as implied in the *Eumenides* of Æschylus.[1] Descending farther, we reached the southern side of the 'Pelasgic wall,' which is covered with multitudes of minutely written inscriptions recording the decrees of the Amphictyons, or of the Delphic community, with a large number specially relating to the manumission of slaves belonging to the temple. It was in examining these inscriptions, under a burning sun, that Otfried Müller spent the last few days of his life,[2] and the work that was then left unfinished was afterwards completed by the labours of the French archæologists, Wescher and Foucart.[3]

From the site of the temple of Apollo, we walked towards the rift between the two great cliffs ; crossed the small stream that comes down the rift, at a point where the washerwomen were in full force ; and so reached a spot where, under a wall of rock, we saw to the right a jet of water

---

[1] *Ibid.* 32, ἐτῶν πάλῳ λαχόντες, ὡς νομίζεται.
[2] E. Curtius, *Alterthum und Gegenwart*, ii 246-260.
[3] Foucart, *Sur l'affranchissement des esclaves*, 1867.

gushing out of a spout into a small tank confined within low walls of stone, and thickly covered with water-weeds. The surroundings have been somewhat altered by the earthquake of 1870; but the tank is none other than the Bath of the Delphic pilgrims, where all who came to consult the oracle purified themselves before entering the sacred precincts; and the water is none other than that of the classic fountain of Castalia. To the Greeks of earlier times it was simply the water of purification; it was only later writers, and especially Roman poets, who fancied that the stream was a source of inspiration to the poet, if not to the Pythian priestess herself.[1] This bath is the theme of the following lines in the *Greek Anthology* (xiv 71), purporting to be a response of the priestess herself:—

ἁγνὸς πρὸς τέμενος καθαρὸν, ξένε, δαίμονος ἔρχου
ψυχὴν, νυμφαίου νάματος ἁψάμενος·
ὡς ἀγαθοῖς κεῖται[2] βαιὴ λιβάς· ἄνδρα δὲ φαῦλον
οὐδ' ἂν ὁ πᾶς νίψαι νάμασιν Ὠκεανός.

---

[1] Ovid, *Amores*, i 15, 35, mihi flavus Apollo pocula Castalia plena ministret aqua; Statius, *Silvæ*, v 5, *init.;* Martial, xii 3, 11; Schol. ad Eur. *Phæn.* 230, Κασταλία ... εἰς ἣν λέγουσι τὰς ἱεροδούλους παρθένους λούεσθαι, μελλούσας θεοπρόπιον φθέγξεσθαι, ἐν τῷ τρίποδι; Lucian, *Jup. Trag.* 30, πηγῆς μαντικῆς, οἵα ἡ Κασταλία ἐστίν (Ulrichs, pp. 57 *f.*)

[2] The correction ἀρκεῖ, proposed by Jacobs, is confirmed by an

> To the pure precincts of Apollo's portal,
>   Come, pure in heart, and touch the lustral wave :
>   One drop sufficeth for the sinless mortal ;
>   All else, e'en ocean's billows cannot lave.

We drank of the water at a point where it was more accessible than at the jet across the tank, and found it as 'sweet to drink' as Pausanias found it (x 8 § 9). We then wandered for a few yards up the dry ravine, over large stones strewn in all directions along the course of the now diminished torrent, under rocks overarching high above our heads. The ravine reminded me of Gordale Scar, near Malham Cove, in the Craven district of Yorkshire.

After this we descended towards the olive-trees near the site of the ancient gymnasium, which is now occupied by the monastery, where travellers sometimes stay for the night. We also visited the neighbouring church with its old Byzantine paintings. The view from the monastery was remarkably fine, and we would gladly have stayed longer to enjoy it. However, at half-past two we

---

improved version of this epigram, quoted in Dübner's edition :—
Σαράπιδος χρησμὸς Τιμαινέτῳ.
> ἁγνὰς χεῖρας ἔχων καὶ νοῦν ἐπὶ γλῶσσαν ἀληθῆ
>   εἴσιθι μὴ λοετροῖς ἀλλὰ νόῳ καθαρός.
> ἀρκεῖ γάρ θ' ὁσίοις ῥανὶς ὕδατος · ἄνδρα δὲ φαῦλον
>   οὐδ' ἂν ὁ πᾶς λούσαι χεύμασιν Ὠκεανός.

began to retrace our steps, and before long reached the commencement of a new carriage road to Sálona, which enabled us to keep for a while on a level route, some distance below the point from which we had first caught sight of Delphi. We then hastened down the rough paths of our morning's climb, reached Chrysó again with comparative ease; and, after losing our way in the intricate streets of the village, found ourselves once more in the open country. Crossing the main road, we lighted on a short cut which we had missed in the morning, and thus, by a steep and irregular zigzag, reached the level of the old Crisæan plain. An hour's walk by a nearly straight path brought us through the welcome shade of the vast olive plantations to the high road between Sálona and the gulf; and we shortly afterwards reached Itéa, after an expedition of ten hours and a half, at half-past six.

The steamer which was to take us away was already in port; so we turned in for our evening meal, and, after paying a bill amounting in all to eleven drachmas and ten lepta (or less than seven shillings), we went by the light of the moon and stars down to the small pier where our host, who had really been very attentive, saw us safely into a boat. To the ordinary words of farewell, καλὴν ἀντάμωσιν (*au revoir*), he replied with a hearty *amen*. Soon after, we were restored to perfect comfort in our cabin on board the *Elpis*, the steamer which we had left at Nauplia, and which had meanwhile been round the whole of the Peloponnesus. We had long gone to rest when the steamer weighed anchor after midnight, reaching Corinth about half-past five in the morning.

V

THE ISTHMIAN GAMES—CORINTH TO ZANTE

γέφυραν ποντιάδα πρὸ Κορίνθου τειχέων.—PINDAR, *Isthmia*, iii 38.
ὑλήεντι Ζακύνθῳ.—*Odyssey*, i 246.

APRIL 9.—After we had breakfasted at the *Hôtel de la Couronne*, I started by myself at eight o'clock, to walk across the Isthmus, and to visit the scene of the Isthmian games. On reaching the highest point of the road, I had a view of the islands and coast of the Saronic Gulf, and then struck off, to the right, towards the village of Hagios Ioannes, passing remains of the Isthmian wall on the way. After about an hour's walk from Corinth, I came upon a small party of land-surveyors; but, on my inquiring, they could only tell me of some ruins near the small white chapel of St. John, and knew nothing of the site of the ancient *stadium*, though all the while they were only separated from it by a bank of earth, as I soon found on reaching the end of the embankment. It lies in a long field parallel to the road, with one of its extremities bounded by a straight line, and the other by what was once a semicircle, but is now much broken by a stream that has worked its way through the bank surrounding its upper end. I counted two hundred and fifty paces from one end to the other; but my steps were shorter than usual, owing to the numbers of large stones strewn over the field.[1] At the upper end were two narrow gullies, up which I walked for a short distance and found several small specimens of the *Pinus Haleppensis*,—the lineal descendants of the trees which once supplied the victor's crown at the Isthmian games. I plucked off a small branch, and retraced my steps, crossed the road, and reached a rude platform of irregular outline with traces of ancient walls around it. A large herd of goats was pasturing on what were once the precincts of the Isthmian sanctuary. Near the chapel, I saw some fragments of Doric columns, and some modern graves covered with heaps of stones taken from the ancient remains, and marked by low crosses of unpainted wood. Beyond it, part of the ancient wall has been excavated to the depth of about ten feet.[2]

[1] The dimensions, as given in Leake's *Morea*, iii 286, are 650 feet.

[2] In Clark's *Peloponnesus* there is a plan of the sacred precincts, which is copied in Bursian's *Geographie*.

After this, I walked along part of the new railway line, saw the modern village of Isthmia, crossed the new canal, which is expected to join the two seas in 1888, reached the station of Kalamaki on the Saronic Gulf at 10.30, and about eleven o'clock returned by train to Corinth.

After lunch we went once more on board the *Elpis* and started at one o'clock for Zante. The waters of the gulf were delightfully calm, and we enjoyed the view of the northern shore as we passed the rugged promontory of the Peræa. Soon afterwards we caught sight of the range of Cithæron towards the east, and looked for the last time on the slopes of Helicon with their belt of gloom, and upon the snowy summits of Parnassus and the mountains beyond Sálona. As the steamer, however, did not stop at any place on the northern coast, we kept nearer to the southern shore, thus enjoying a series of fine views of the lofty ranges of Achaia and Arcadia, which are separated from the coast by only a narrow fringe of alluvial soil. The rocky ravines and the intricately interlacing glens were at their finest just before we reached our first stopping place at Vostitza, or Ægium, which is delightfully situated on hilly slopes, with winding roads connecting the upper and lower parts of the town. Along the shore is a range of cliffs mantled with verdure and watered with rivulets, while the harbour is so deep that vessels of large size can lie at anchor close to the land. After this, the views became less interesting as we approached the narrower part of the gulf, and it was already dark when we passed between the two lighthouses that mark the forts of Rhium and Antirrhium. When we reached Patras, about eight o'clock, we could only see the long lines of its brilliantly lighted streets extending above one another parallel to the shore.

April 10.—It was not until five in the morning that our steamer started again, passing, at some distance to the north, Missolonghi, and the Oxia islands where the battle was fought which takes its usual name from the Turkish naval station of Lepanto within the gulf of Corinth. Soon after, I had a distant glimpse of Ithaca, and a nearer view of the far larger island of Cephalonia. About 8.30 the steamer stopped at Clarenza, which stands on the mainland a few miles north of the Frankish castle of Khlemoutzi. The latter looked like a large martello tower crowning the crest of a rocky promontory projecting from the plain of Elis.

We reached Zante about half-past ten and put up at the *Albergo Nazionale*, a clean and comfortable hotel, where our room overlooks a small piazza paved with smooth stones of almost dazzling brightness.

In the afternoon, we walked through the principal street of the town with long colonnades resembling, on a humbler scale, those of Bologna, and with one or two small palaces built in the Venetian style of the Renaissance. On getting out into the country we went on for an hour along a road fringed with olive-trees and bright with wayside flowers, till we reached a spot called Kalamaki, on the bay of Keri. The bay forms an irregular crescent with high ground at both ends and with two islands between.

April 11.—We walked along the esplanade and past the picturesque harbour, looking all the while at a bay of brilliant blue, from whose shores rose more than one graceful campanile which distantly reminded us of Venice. The town lies along this bay, between two heights—that of the Castle-hill rising 350 feet to the north-west, and that of Skopós (the ancient *Elatos*), rising 1300 feet to the south-east. At two o'clock we started to climb the latter, but, owing to the broken ground and the many smaller hills which surround it, the way proved rather more intricate than we expected. At last we had to scramble up a rough hillside along thorny tracks that were fit for goats alone, while the goats themselves were placidly feeding among lavender blossoms on the level ground below. However, a country girl came down to meet us, and, from a ruined chapel that we soon reached, guided us along winding paths by bushes of myrtle, until, after half an hour's further climb, we reached the monastery of Mount Skopós. Here we were invited up into a large room, from whose windows we had a wonderful view of the town and bay far below, and the island of Cephalonia, with its Black Mountain, beyond ten miles of sea. The actual summit of Skopós is only a few minutes farther, at the top of a craggy knob of bare rock, which proved rougher climbing than any we had had on that afternoon. From the summit we saw the coast of Elis, while below us lay the bay of Keri. At five o'clock we went back with our guide to the point where we first met her, when her place was taken by her elder sister—a strong and handsome girl, with black hair and a bronzed complexion—who, while leading us down the intricate paths of our descent, told me a long story of some Englishmen who, like us, had lost their way, and were actually benighted on the hill. I cannot say that I succeeded in following all the details of the story, and it was like a light shining in a dark place that I occasionally caught some clear and completely intelligible phrase, such as ἀνήψαμεν τὸ φῶς, a bit of pure old Greek that would have been understood with equal certainty at any time in the last two thousand years and more. But, side by side with Greek like this, she always used, instead of the ordinary ναί for 'yes,' the exceptional form ναίσκε, which, however, reminded one of the old form ναίχι that occurs in an epigram of Callimachus, which is not without interest in its bearing on a point of Greek pronunciation.[1] As soon as we had no further need of her guidance, she left us with hearty farewells, and in the twilight vanished up the hill. The moon was already shining when we got back at half-past seven.

April 12.—It was a gusty morning, and we stayed indoors. In the afternoon we had the pleasure of making the acquaintance of Mr. Alfred L. Crowe, Consular Agent of the United States. He kindly took us for a walk up the Castle-hill, past the church and palm-tree which form one of

---

[1] Λυσανίη, σὺ δὲ ναίχι καλός, καλός, ἀλλὰ πρὶν εἰπεῖν τοῦτο σαφῶς, ἠχώ φησί τις ἄλλον ἔχειν. Here ἔχει ἄλλος is an echo of ναίχι καλός, and αι becomes ε (Geldart's *Modern Greek*, p. 26). ναίχι is also found in Soph. *O. T.* 682, and elsewhere. It will be observed that the echo is regardless of the accent of καλός. The epigram may be found in *Anth. Pal.* xii 43 = Callimachus, *Ep.* 30 (28).

the illustrations in Lady Brassey's *Sunshine and Storm in the East*,[1] and onwards, with ever varying prospects of the plain and the hills of Zante, to his former home, with its orchard full of orange-trees, some of them laden with fruit, and others fragrant with blossom. After passing through large plantations of olive-trees, we reached his charming summer resort, in the midst of a garden brilliant with innumerable flowers, and on the verge of a cliff looking down on the sea and across to the coast of Elis.

[1] P. 131.

VI

OLYMPIA

ἵκοντο δ' ὑψηλοῖο πέτραν ἀλίβατον Κρονίου.
PINDAR, *Olympia*, vi 64.

APRIL 13.—At 8 P.M. on the previous evening we had gone on board the Panhellenic steamer *Athene*, with a view to starting for Katákolon, the port for Olympia, early the next morning. It was not, however, until six o'clock in the morning that our steamer left the harbour, and consequently it was nearly nine before we reached Katákolon. On arriving, we were hurried off the steamer by the eagerness of some boatmen who were anxious for a fare, and, on landing, we found that the first train for Pyrgos, which is a little more than a third of the way to Olympia, had already started at eight, and that the next train was at 11.30. As there was no conveyance to be had, we were obliged to wait in an aimless way at this desolate place, within sight of the hospitable steamer (which waited for some hours in the harbour), and without any chance of breakfast on land, except a few oranges. Our train took half an hour to accomplish the seven and a half miles to Pyrgos, and, on arriving, at noon, we at once got into an open carriage with two horses and drove to Olympia. (The distance is twelve miles, and the fare twenty drachmæ, which is little more than twelve shillings.) On our way we crossed the Enipeus, after which we ascended by long windings to the loftily situated village of Smyla, where we had an extensive view of the low hills of Elis and some of the higher Arcadian ranges beyond.

We reached Olympia at three, and at first were somewhat disappointed to find that Georgios Pliris had established himself at the foot of the hill of Druva, instead of at the top, as the guide-book had led us to expect. Georgios, who was formerly cook to the German explorers of Olympia, produced a Greek testimonial to his efficiency signed by Professor Treu and others, and showed us our room, a most unpretentious apartment, adorned with small photographs of the Crown Prince of Prussia, Ernst Curtius, and others. After this his son, a bright and modest lad, showed us the way to the ruins. We crossed the Kladeos by a plank, and then walked past a few olive-trees to the pine-clad hill of Kronos. Pindar, by an almost pardonable flourish of poetic exaggeration, describes this hill as ὑψηλὸς and ἀλίβατος; but, although steep in parts, it is only 123 metres, or 403 feet, above the level of the sea. Its original height, however, has apparently been diminished by a landslip, which covered the ground for some distance from its base with a layer of marl a foot thick, and thus preserved for us the Hermes of Praxiteles.

On a spur projecting from the lowest ledge of this famous hill we paused under the shadow of two pine-trees to survey the scene of the Olympic festival. Here we saw immediately before us, to the south, the sacred enclosure of the Altis, 219 yards long by 190 broad, bounded by the wall of unexcavated soil, and strewn with what at first sight resembled a perfect chaos of blocks of stone. Soon, however, we were able to distinguish, immediately below us, the remains of the *Heræum*, which is not only the oldest temple of Olympia, but the oldest Greek temple yet discovered. Beyond this is the faintly marked pentagonal precinct of the *Pelopion;* then the lofty platform and the broad bases of the columns of the great temple of Zeus. Immediately to our right are the ruins of the *Prytaneion*, with the banquet-hall of the Olympic victors. South of this is the *Philippeion*, a circular building erected by Philip of Macedon after his victory at Chæronea, and (outside the Altis) the *gymnasium* and *palæstra;* while to our left is the semicircular *exedra* of Herodes Atticus. To the left of this, again, are the remains of the series of treasure-houses, so elaborately described by Pausanias, which once enshrined the votive offerings of many of the cities of the Hellenic world— Megara, Sikyon, Gela, Selinus, Metapontum, and others; to the south of these, the temple dedicated to the Mother of the Gods; and to the east of them, the entrance to the *stadium*. All these and many other ruined remains were bounded to the west by the deep bed of the Kladeos, and to the south by the broad Alpheus, with a range of low hills beyond it. After this general survey we descended into the Altis and visited, among many other points, the entrance to the *stadium*, where we saw the line of flat stones that marked the starting-point of the foot-race. The exact length of this *stadium* has been ascertained to be 192.27 metres, or 630.8 feet, thus giving us, as its six hundredth part, .3205 metres [1] as the length of the Olympic foot, which is the unit of measurement in many of the buildings at Olympia. After wan-

---

[1] Or 1.05015 English feet, *i.e.* little more than three-fifths of an inch longer than an English foot.

dering over the rest of the ruins, we returned at dusk to our quarters at the foot of the hill of Druva.

April 14.—On the side of the Kladeos opposite to the Altis, a large museum has been erected which, in due time, will contain all the remains of ancient art discovered during the excavations. At present these are scattered over several sheds which we now proceeded to visit. We began with the museum of bronzes, in the first room of which, among numerous fragments of marble sculpture, we saw the famous Hermes of Praxiteles, which is much the most important statue that has come to light during the excavations, and looks far more beautiful in the original marble than in any of the reproductions of it which are to be seen in the museums of Europe. In the same room is the colossal head of Hera sculptured in the soft yellowish limestone of the district.[1] Among the most interesting of the inscriptions that have been discovered, is a dedication to the Olympic Zeus by Mummius, the destroyer of Corinth;[2] also the base of a statue in honour of the historian Poly-

---

[1] Engraved in Bötticher's *Olympia*, p. 237, ed. 1; Baumeister's *Denkmäler*, p. 1087.

[2] Λεύκιος Μόμμιος Λευκίου υἱὸς στρατηγὸς ὕπατος Ῥωμαίων Διὶ Ὀλυμπίῳ.

bius;[1] and another inscribed by one of the quartermasters of Alexander the Great.[2] The bronzes include a spear-head which was part of the spoils dedicated to the Olympic Zeus by the people of Tarentum, on their victory over Thurii (B.C. 440-430).[3] Also a life-sized head of an Olympic boxer of somewhat brutal physiognomy.[4] And, lastly, a rectangular plaque bearing four sets of reliefs ranged above one another, the lowest being a winged Artemis of an oriental type, holding up two lions by their hind legs; the next, Hercules kneeling while aiming an arrow at a retreating centaur; above this, two griffins facing one another; and, at the top, three eagles. The whole work is a most suggestive record of the gradual development of Greek art, and a remarkable instance of the influence exercised upon it by the art of Assyria.[5]

We next proceeded to the museum of terracottas, with its most interesting remains of various architectural ornaments. We then entered the

---

[1] ἡ πόλις τῶν Ἠλείων Πολύβιον Λυκόρτα Μεγαλοπολείτην.

[2] βασιλέως Ἀλε[ξάνδρου] ἡμεροδρόμας καὶ βηματιστὴς τῆς Ἀσίας κ.τ.λ. Hicks, *Greek Historical Inscriptions*, No. 129.

[3] Σκῦλα ἀπὸ Θουρίων Ταραντῖνοι ἀνέθηκαν Διῒ Ὀλυμπίῳ δεκάταν.

[4] Bötticher, p. 334; Baumeister, p. 1087.

[5] Bötticher, p. 181, ed. 1; reproduced in Förster's *Olympia*, p. 9. There is a cast of this 'plaque, with repoussée work and engraved figures,' in the South Kensington Museum of Antique Casts, No. 5.

museum of sculpture, a badly lighted shed, on the floor of which were strewn the fragmentary statues from the eastern and western pediments of the temple of Zeus, the former, by Paiônios, representing the preparations for the contest of Pelops with Œnomaos for the hand of his daughter Hippodameia; and the latter, by Alcamenes, one of the ablest contemporaries of Pheidias, with a highly spirited representation of the battle of the centaurs and Lapithæ at the marriage of Peirithoos.[1] In the same shed is the fine Metope with the burly Atlas bringing the apples of the Hesperides to Hercules, who is meanwhile bending his head downward to bear the weight of all the heavens, in the form of what can only be described as a small pillow, which one of the Hesperides, standing behind him, is pretending to support by thrusting her upturned wrist against it.[2] Here also there was to be seen, lying on the ground, the beautiful piece of marble drapery belonging to the Hermes of Praxiteles; and, in the same inglorious position, the upper part of the noble form of the Niké of Paiônios, which requires to be seen on a lofty pedestal in the open air before its majesty can be duly appreciated. This statue was the first im-

[1] Newton's *Essays*, p. 354-365.
[2] Bötticher, p. 285, ed. 1; Förster, p. 22; Baumeister, p. 1081.

portant discovery of the German expedition. In the fine phrase of a Transatlantic poet,

'The herald Niké, first,
From the dim resting-place unfettered burst,
Winged victor over fate and time and death!'[1]

As one looked at all these scattered fragments of badly lighted and ill-arranged sculptures, one could hardly help feeling that, until they were all properly placed in the new museum, it was far easier and more profitable to study and enjoy them in such a gallery as the Cambridge Museum of Classical Archæology, or the Museum of antique casts at South Kensington. On emerging from one of these gloomy sheds, we saw drooping over it a judas-tree with its leafless branches completely covered with a magnificent mass of pink blossom.[2]

We then visited the ruins once more, and saw the pedestal of the Niké, with its two inscriptions: (1) its original dedication by the Messenians, probably in memory of the capture of Pylos in 425 B.C.;[3] (2) the record of the decision of the dispute as to boundaries between the Lacedæ-

---

[1] E. C. Stedman, *News from Olympia*. Newton's *Essays*, p. 353.
[2] *Cercis siliquastrum*, Sibthorp's *Flora Græca*, iv 60, figure 367.
[3] Μεσσάνιοι καὶ Ναυπάκτιοι ἀνέθεν Διῒ 'Ολυμπίῳ δεκάταν ἀπὸ τῶμ πολεμίων. Παιώνιος ἐποίησε Μενδαῖος· καὶ τἀκρωτήρια ποιῶν ἐπὶ τὸν ναὸν ἐνίκα (Hicks, No. 49).

monians and Messenians, three centuries later.[1] Also the pedestal of the statue of Zeus set up by the Lacedæmonians on the 'second revolt' of the Messenians, still bearing (with slight discrepancies) the inscription recorded by Pausanias (v 24 § 3)[2]; that of the Bull of Philesios dedicated by the Eretrians (27 § 9); and lastly that of a statue of an athlete by Pythagoras of Rhegium.

In the afternoon, we walked past the hill of Kronos along a sandy footpath up the valley of the Alpheus on the way to Arcadia. We noticed to our right the stone slabs that mark the goal of the *stadium*, most of the interval between this point and the starting-place consisting of unexcavated ground that was waving with green blades of corn. As we wandered along, we had lovely views of the low hills that fringe the valley of the Alpheus, which is very variable in its breadth and in many parts has a broad dry bed of sand far wider than the actual stream. About a mile above the scene of the Olympic games, we crossed a small brook, and, on the grassy slope beyond, saw the site of the ancient Pisa. About the same distance farther up the valley, we ascended a small

---

[1] Referred to by Tacitus, *Ann.* iv 43; Hicks, pp. 341-344.

[2] [Δέξο ἄνα]ξ Κρονίδα [Ζ]εῦ 'Ολύνπιε καλὸν ἄγαλμα ἰλήῳ [θυ]μῷ τῷ Λακεδαιμονίῳ. Cf. Thuc. i 101-103 (Hicks, No. 17).

hill which lies between the path and the river, and is called the 'hill of the suitors,'—the legendary spot described by Pausanias as the burial-place of the unsuccessful suitors for the hand of Hippodameia.[1] We sat down for a while under the pines on its summit, where we found a small tortoise, which we would gladly have brought back with us as a memento of our visit; but, after all, it would hardly have been a fitting memorial of the place where the crown was awarded for swiftness of foot, and, on our return, we carried off a more appropriate remembrance of the scene by plucking a sprig of olive from the trees beside the hill of Kronos.

In the evening we climbed the little hill of Druva, 374 feet above the level of the plain, mounting the slopes by paths scooped out by water-courses, until we passed the house of the *Ephoros*, which was built for the German explorers high above the valley, where the malaria is dangerous during the summer season. After threading our way through the cottages of the hamlet at the top, we went by a track between the furrows of a flourishing cornfield to the neighbouring outlook of Monteverde, where there was a fine panorama

[1] vi 21 § 9, γῆς χῶμα ὑψηλόν, τῶν μνηστήρων τῆς Ἱπποδαμείας τάφος.

of mountains to the east and north, while to the south we looked across the Alpheus toward the wooded hills which were the retreat of Xenophon during his twenty years of exile.[1] To the west we could follow the lower reaches of the river till it fell into the sea, beyond which the islands of Zante and Cephalonia could be discerned on the distant horizon.

April 15.—We rose before five and started by carriage for Pyrgos soon after six. The rain of the previous night had cleared the air, and the morning was fresh and cool. By the roadside we saw numbers of yellow irises and asphodels. The latter is perhaps the most disenchanting plant in the classic flora.[2] It is a tall kind of lily, with long ragged leaves, and spikes of flowers of a faintly purple hue. It will grow almost anywhere in waste places; so that the 'mead of asphodel,' in which Homer's heroes are described as pacing to and fro in the unseen world, would seem to imply a barren waste where other plants would hardly grow, and may perhaps find its closest

---

[1] *Anabasis* v 3 § 7; *Hell.* vi 5 § 2. Temple of Athene dedicated by him, Pausanias, v 6 §§ 4-7; vi 22 § 4.

[2] See Sibthorp's *Flora Græca*, iv 28, figure 334; Welcker's *Tagebuch*, i 171; Mure's *Tour*, ii 261; and Tozer's *Lectures*, 162.

parallel in the forlorn and desolate region which Virgil calls the *loca senta situ*.

After crossing the Enipeus, we walked uphill to the highest point of the road, near the village of Palaio-Barbasena, where we enjoyed an extensive view. We reached Pyrgos after nine, left by the train at 9.30, arrived at Katákolon at ten, went on board the steamer at noon, started at 1.45, and, in about three hours, amid rain and thunder and lightning, crossed over again to Zante.

VII

ZANTE TO CORFU

ἀμφιλαφὴς πίειρα Κεραυνίῃ εἰν ἁλὶ νῆσος .
APOLLONIUS RHODIUS, iv 982.

APRIL 16.—A rainy day. In the afternoon we walked up the Castle-hill and down into the plain of Zante, with its delightful olive yards and orange gardens.

April 17.—About eleven o'clock we left Zante for Corfu, by the Panhellenic company's steamer *Hermupolis*. The hill of Skopós remained long in sight, and after a few hours we reached Cephalonia—a bare island with rugged hills, and little, if any, sign of water. The top of its highest point, the Black Mountain, was covered with clouds. After landing passengers at two places, Lixouri and the capital of the island, Argostoli, we waited for more than an hour in the large land-locked harbour, and it was five o'clock before we started again.

After midnight I saw, through the port-hole of my cabin, a long spit of land which was part of Paxos, the island associated with the singular story told by Plutarch in his treatise on the cessation of oracles, as to the pilot who, while sailing towards Italy, heard a voice near this island calling him aloud by name in the dead of night, and bidding him, in the bay of Buthrotum, for which he was bound, proclaim that the great god Pan was dead.[1] When he reached the bay his vessel was becalmed, and he was fain to cry aloud that Pan was dead, 'wherewithal there were such piteous outcrys and dreadful shrieking as hath not been the like.'[2]

[1] *De defectu oraculorum*, xvi. οὗτος ἔφη ποτὲ πλέων εἰς Ἰταλίαν ἐπιβῆναι νεώς, ἐμπορικὰ χρήματα καὶ συχνοὺς ἐπιβάτας ἀγούσης· ἑσπέρας δὲ ἤδη περὶ τὰς Ἐχινάδας νήσους ἀποσβῆναι τὸ πνεῦμα, καὶ τὴν ναῦν διαφερομένην πλησίον γενέσθαι Παξῶν· ... ἐξαίφνης δὲ φωνὴν ἀπὸ τῆς νήσου τῶν Παξῶν ἀκουσθῆναι, Θαμοῦν τινὸς βοῇ καλοῦντος, ὥστε θαυμάζειν. ὁ δὲ Θαμοῦς Αἰγύπτιος ἦν κυβερνήτης, οὐδὲ τῶν ἐμπλεόντων γνώριμος πολλοῖς ἀπ' ὀνόματος· δὶς μὲν οὖν κληθέντα σιωπῆσαι, τὸ δὲ τρίτον ὑπακοῦσαι τῷ καλοῦντι· κἀκεῖνον ἐπιτείναντα τὴν φωνὴν εἰπεῖν ὅτι "Ὅταν γένῃ κατὰ τὸ Παλῶδες, ἀπάγγειλον, ὅτι Πὰν ὁ μέγας τέθνηκε ... ὡς οὖν ἐγένετο κατὰ τὸ Παλῶδες, οὔτε πνεύματος ὄντος, οὔτε κλύδωνος, ἐκ πρύμνης βλέποντα τὸν Θαμοῦν πρὸς τὴν γῆν εἰπεῖν, ὅτι ὁ μέγας Πὰν τέθνηκεν. οὒ φθῆναι δὲ παυσάμενον αὐτόν, καὶ γενέσθαι μέγαν οὐχ ἑνός, ἀλλὰ πολλῶν στεναγμὸν ἅμα θαυμασμῷ μεμιγμένον. Cf. Eusebius, *Præparatio Evangelica*, v chaps 16-17.

[2] Old commentator on Spenser's *Pastorals in May*, quoted in T. Warton's note on Milton's *Nativity Ode*, xx. Cf. George Sandys, *A Relation of a Journey begun An. Dom. 1610*, p. 11, ed. 1615, who, like Milton in 1629, connects the story with the cessa-

The legend is embalmed in the melodious lines of Milton,—

> 'The lonely mountains o'er,
> And the resounding shore,
> A voice of weeping heard and loud lament;'

and also in *The Dead Pan* of Mrs. Browning,—

> 'And that dismal cry rose slowly,
> And sank slowly through the air,
> Full of spirit's melancholy
> And eternity's despair!
> And they heard the words it said,—
> "Pan is dead,—Great Pan is dead,—
> Pan, Pan is dead."'

April 18.—About five in the morning we reached Corfu, and were apprised of the fact by the porter of the *Hôtel de St. Georges* knocking loudly at our cabin door. In the forenoon we walked to the south along the Marina under the shade of trees, until we reached a peninsula between two bays—that of Kastrades, towards the sea, and that of Khalikhiópulo, towards the land. This peninsula is the site of the ancient Corcyra, and still preserves the name of *Palæopolis*. At its farthest extremity, from a point called 'the one-gun

---

tion of oracles, and ends his version of it with the words: 'forthwith there was heard a great *lamentation*, accompanied with grones and skreeches.'

battery,' we enjoyed a delightfully varied view. To the right lies the bay that was one of the harbours of Corcyra.[1] In front is the low ground, watered by streams, that is imagined to be the spot where Odysseus landed and met Nausicaa. The quaint little island, crowned with cypresses, to the left, is one of the two islands fancifully identified as the Phæacian vessel which bore Odysseus home to Ithaca, and on its return was transformed into stone by the wrath of Poseidon (*Odyssey*, xiii 161). Across the ferry, just before us, are a series of hills and headlands clothed with the richest verdure.

On our return we soon mounted up, through olive groves, to the small church of the Ascension, where there is a fine view of the mountains of the mainland. We then descended toward the coast, where we saw the scanty remains of a small Doric temple beautifully placed in a little dell overlooking the sea.[2]

At eleven o'clock, from the windows of our room, we saw, passing along the esplanade, one of the three great annual processions in honour of St. Spyridion, the patron saint of Corfu. There were groups of country people in bright costumes looking on, and a long line of priests in gorgeous

---

[1] The λιμὴν 'Υλλαϊκός of Thucydides, iii 72 § 3; 81 § 2.
[2] Bursian, *Geogr.* ii 360, note 2.

robes marching in front with a canopy, under which were the relics of the saint.

Thanks to a kind letter of introduction from Sir Patrick Colquhoun, formerly Chief Justice of the Ionian Islands, we made the acquaintance of Dr. Palatiano, who has long been resident in Corfu. In the afternoon he accompanied us on a drive to the loftily situated village of Pelleka, seven or eight miles distant on the west side of the island. Owing to the good tradition of English rule, the island still enjoys excellent roads, which are kept in repair by means of a tax upon oil. Our road passed between high hedges of cactus and through vast groves of fine old olive-trees. From the top of the hill above Pelleka we enjoyed a magnificent view extending over Santa Deka and other hills to the south, and Monte Salvatore and the lofty Pass of Pantaleone to the north. Below us were the waters of the Adriatic, while a large part of the island was spread out like a map before us.

On our return, among some trees near the Strada Marina, we were shown the celebrated cenotaph of Menecrates—a round structure built of small pieces of limestone let into a shallow trench, and bearing an inscription consisting of six hexameter lines, in characters of peculiar epigraphic interest, belonging to the early part of the sixth century B.C.[1]

We spent the evening with the family of Dr. Palatiano, where I learnt much that was interesting about modern Greek education, and where we unavoidably fell into a discussion as to the various methods of pronouncing Greek, and as to the conflicting claims of quantity and accent. Much of the school training appears to consist of paraphrasing the terse language of ancient Greek into the prolix modern style. The servant who brought in the tea was a picturesque old man who, strange to say, had actually fought in his youth in the war of the Greek independence, and during that war had been for several years a prisoner among the Turks.

April 19.—In the afternoon we walked to the summit of the citadel to view the panorama of the town and island and the coast of Epirus. The citadel stands on one of the twin peaks, or κορυφαί, that give the place its modern name. On our return we visited the former residence of the Lords Commissioners of the Ionian Islands, where we saw the fine marble lioness found at the tomb

---

[1] Ross, *Archäologische Aufsätze*, ii 563-575; Kaibel's *Epigrammata*, No. 179; facsimile in Roehl's *Inscr. Gr. Antiquissimæ*, 1882, No. 342, and *Imagines*, 1883, p. 61.

of Menecrates—a bold and vigorous piece of workmanship.[1]

After this we had a most enjoyable drive through the olive-groves to Benizze, a village lying on the coast a few miles to the south, surrounded by plantations of orange and lemon-trees. We here saw the remains of a Roman villa with a tesselated pavement, which was partly broken up and covered with water.

April 20.—Our last day in Greece. Early in the forenoon we went on board the Austrian Lloyd steamer *Ceres*, bound for Trieste. Our original plan had been to go by the Rubattino steamer to Brindisi, and along the Italian coast to Venice; but this had to be abandoned, owing to the reported prevalence of cholera at Brindisi, Venice, and Padua, and the inconvenience that was likely to arise in the event of our getting into quarantine. We therefore determined to return by Trieste, Vienna, Munich, Nuremberg, Frankfort, and down the Rhine from Mainz to Rotterdam, and then by the Harwich route to Cambridge, in time for the beginning of term on the 30th of April.

Meanwhile, as our steamer would not start for several hours, we had ample leisure to enjoy the

---

[1] Engraved in Overbeck's *Geschichte der griechischen Plastik*, p 144, ed. 1881; and in Collignon's *Archéologie Grecque*, p. 28.

view of the harbour and the hills of Corfu. Late in the afternoon we steamed away to the north, and as we passed into the open Adriatic, along the Acroceraunian mountains, we watched the twin heights of the citadel—the *aerias Phæacum arces* of Virgil—fading swiftly away in the distance. Thus, among many pleasant memories of our tour, our Easter vacation in Greece came, all too soon, to its inevitable end.

> Farewell to all the classic land,
> The fame-encircled Attic strand :—
> August Athena's matchless fane ;
> Colonus mid the olive-plain ;
> The streams that whisper to the breeze
> Of Plato and of Sophocles ;
> And Daphne's pass, and Deo's shrine,
> And Phyle's fort, and Laurium's mine,
> And wave-washed Sunium's temple lone,
> Mendeli's crest, and Marathon ;
> And Saron's waves that proudly kiss
> The storied shores of Salamis.
>
> Farewell, Ægina's columned steep,
> And Hydra's crag, and Nauplia's keep ;
> And giant walls of Tiryns olden,
> And Agamemnon's city golden.
>
> Farewell to Nemea's flowery dell,
> And Corinth's craggy citadel,
> And Helicon, the Muses' mount,
> And Delphi and Castalia's fount ;

And all the memory-haunted vale
Where Kladeos flows past olives pale
And gray old fanes, that once again
See sunlight on Olympia's plain.
Farewell to all the flowers of Zante,
Fair-smiling *fior di Levante;*
And bright Corfu, whose castles twain
Gleam o'er the dark Ionian main.

Land of the mountains and the sea,
O rock-girt home of Liberty;
Land of green vales and summits hoary,
O sacred shrine of deathless Glory;
   Farewell.

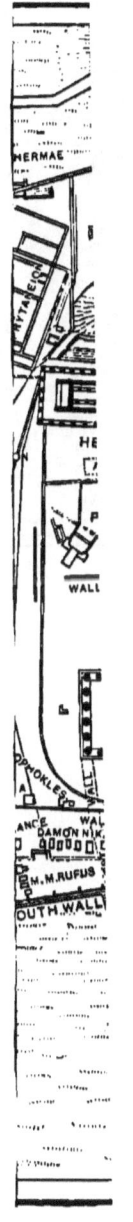

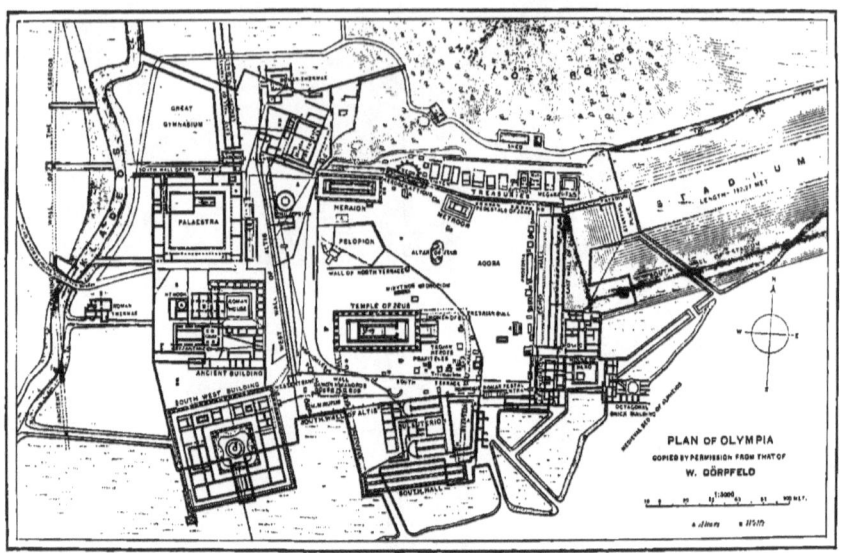

APPENDIX I

BOOKS ON GREEK TRAVEL AND TOPOGRAPHY

Some of the more portable volumes, which are likely to be useful or interesting to travellers in Greece, are marked thus †.

Some of the more important Books of Reference are indicated by an asterisk *.

The modern Greek names of places are printed in italics. The orthography of such names has, to some extent, been made uniform ; but in the case of Colonel Leake's travels, his own spelling has been retained. Leake's principle was not to transliterate the modern Greek characters, but to reproduce the actual pronunciation by the nearest English equivalent. Thus he represents what is usually spelt *Achladó-kampos* by *Akhladhókambo*.

TRAVELS IN GREECE.

Pausanias [*floruit*, 174 A.D.]; ed. Schubart, 2 vols. post 8vo, Leipzig (Teubner), 1862†; ed. L. Dindorf, with Latin translation, royal 8vo, Paris (Didot), 1845.

'The περίοδος Παυσανιακή, or Pausaniac tour of Greece, might still be recommended, as forming a very convenient plan of travels through this country ; namely, from Athens through the Megaris to Corinth ; from thence by Sicyon and Phlius to Argos ; round the Argolis peninsula again to Argos ; from Argos to Sparta ; round the eastern Laconic peninsula again to Sparta ; round the western Laconic peninsula into Messenia ; from Messenia into the Eleia and Achaia ; and lastly, the tour of Arcadia, requiring various deviations. After having returned to Athens, the traveller might follow Pausanias to Eleutherae, to Plataea, and Thebes ; and from thence make the tour of Bœotia and Phocis.' Leake, quoted in Murray's *Greece*, i 93, ed. 1884.

Pausaniae descriptio arcis Athenarum; ed. Otto Jahn ;

ed. altera recognita ab Adolpho Michaelis, aucta cum aliis tabulis tum forma arcis ab I. A. Kaupert descripta. Bonn (Marcus), 1880.†

A. Kalkmann; *Pausanias der Perieget.* Untersuchungen über seine Schriftstellerei und seine Quellen, 8vo, pp. 295.
[Berlin (Reimer), 1886.

Cyriacus of Ancona. Travelled in Greece, chiefly to collect inscriptions; was at Athens in 1437 and 1448, and also visited Delphi. His manuscript collections are now in the Museum at Berlin.

On the visits to Athens by the **Anonymus Viennensis** (circa 1460), **Carrey** (1673), and others, between the Fall of Constantinople in 1453, and Morosini's abandonment of Athens in 1688, see Laborde's *Athènes;* and Michaelis, *der Parthenon*, pp. 334-347.

Sandys, George [1577-1644; translator of Ovid's *Metamorphoses*, etc.] *Relation of a Journey in the Turkish Empire, begun An. Dom.* 1610. Folio, London, 1615; ed. 9, 1673.

> Sailed by Corfu and Santa Maura to Zante, and by Delos to Chios, Lesbos, and Smyrna, and by the Troad to Constantinople, etc.

Transfeldt, J. G. [1648-1700; at Athens, 1674-76]. *Examen reliquarum antiquitatum Atheniensium*, published by A. Michaelis in 'Mittheilungen der Deutschen Archäologischen Instituts in Athen,' vol. i.

Spon, Jacques [1647-1685; a physician of Lyons], et George **Wheler**. *Voyage d'Italie, de Dalmatie, de Grèce et du Levant, fait aux années*, 1675 et 1676. 3 vols. 12mo, Lyons, 1678; 2 vols., Amsterdam, 1679, and La Haye, 1724.

> Vol. I. Corfu—Ithaca—Santa Maura—Zante—by the Strophades and Sphacteria, and past Cythera, to Delos—Myconos—Chios—Tenedos, and through the Troad to Constantinople.
> Vol. II. Zante to Clarenza—Patras—Lepanto—Delphi—Livadia—Thebes—Athens—Salamis—Gulf of Ægina—Eleusis—Megara—Corinth—Athens—Marathon—the Euripus—Thebes—Livadia—*Turco-chório*. Here Spon left by *Dalla—Dístomo* and *Aspraspítia* for Zante and Lyons; while Wheler went on

to *Thálanda*, Lake Copais, Thespiæ, *Kochla* (near Platæa), *Pigadia* (= *Kryo-pegadi* ?), Helicon, and by *Aspraspítia* to Zante, and thence through Italy and France to England, reaching Canterbury in November 1676.

Wheler, G. [1650-1723/24]. *A Journey into Greece by George Wheler, Esq., in company of Dr. Spon of Lyons, in six books, containing*—(1), *A Voyage from Venice to Constantinople;* (2) *An Account of Constantinople and the Adjacent Places;* (3) *A Voyage through the Lesser Asia;* (4) *A Voyage from Zante through several parts of Greece to Athens;* (5) *An Account of Athens;* (6) *Several Journeys from Athens into Attica, Corinth, Bœotia, etc.; with variety of sculptures.* Small folio, London, 1682.

Wheler was born at Breda, in Holland; became a commoner of Lincoln College, Oxford, in 1667; was knighted and ordained in 1683; was prebendary of Durham, 1684; afterwards vicar of Basingstoke, and rector of Houghton-le-Spring. The greater part of his work is practically a translation of that of his fellow-traveller, Spon; with the addition of some plates of 'curious plants,' a map of Achaia, and 'divers medals and other antiquities.'

Vernon, F. Letter to H. Oldenburg in *Philosophical Transactions*, xi, No. 124. April 24, 1676.

Brown, E., M.D. *Travels.* pp. 34-54, 'The description of Larissa and Thessaly.' London, 1685.

Randolph, B. *The Present State of the Morea; with a description of Athens, Zant, Strafades, and Serigo*, pp. 26, ed. 3. London, 1689.

Drummond, A., *Travels in Germany, Greece, Asia Minor, to the Euphrates.* Folio, London, 1754.

pp. 94-114. Zante—Myconos—Delos—Smyrna.

Bartholdy, J. L. S. *Voyage en Grèce*, 1803-4. 2 vols. 8vo [translated from the German], Paris, 1807.

Pouqueville, F. C. H. L. *Voyage en Morée, Constantinople, en Albanie, etc.*, 3 vols. 8vo, Paris, 1805. *Voyage dans la Grèce*, 5 vols. 8vo, Paris, 1820.

Chandler, R. [1738-1810]; Fellow of Magdalen College,

Oxford. *Travels in Greece ; or, an Account of a Tour made at the Expense of the Society of Dilettanti.* 4to, Oxford, 1776.

20th August 1765. Smyrna—Carystus—Sunium—Ægina—Athens and Attica. Megara—Isthmus of Corinth—Methana—Ægina — Salamis. Peiræus — *Poros* — Methana — Trœzen — *Damalá* — Epidaurus—*Ligurio*—Nauplia—Tiryns—Argos—Mycenæ—Nemea—Cleonæ—Corinth—the Isthmus—Corinth to Anticyra.—*Distomo*—Stiris—Bulis—Ascra—Helicon. From *Distomo* by the Schisté to Delphi. Thence to the port and to *Galixidi*—*Vostitza*—Patrás—the Echinades—*Clarenza*—*Gastouni*—Elis —Olympia—*Miráka*. [Account of the journey of M. Bocher, a French architect at Zante, to *Vernizza*, and his discovery of the Temple of Apollo at Bassæ in November 1765.] *Clarenza* (July 1766)—Zante (September). Thence to Venice and Bristol.

Scrofani, X. *Voyage en Grèce* (1794-95). Trans. from the Italian. 3 vols., Paris, 1801.

Stephanopoli, D. and M. *Voyage en Grèce*, 1797-98. 2 vols. 8vo, London, 1800.

Sonnini, C. S. *Voyage en Grèce et en Turquie.* 2 vols. 8vo, Paris, 1801.

Dodwell, E. [1767-1832]. *A Classical and Topographical Tour through Greece, during the years* 1801, 1805, *and* 1806. 2 vols. 4to, 70 plates, London, 1819.

Vol. I. *First Tour*, 27th May 1801. Corfu—Leukas—*Prévesa* — Ithaca — Cephalonia — Patrás (and by Phocis and Bœotia to Athens).
Second Tour, 3d February 1805. *Zante*—*Mesolongi*—*Galaxidi* —*Sálona* — Delphi—*Distomo* — *Aráchova* — Daulis — Panopeus —*Livadia* — Chæroneia — Orchomenos—Lake Copais—*Romaikó* —*Granitza*—back to *Livadia*—Haliartos—Thespiæ—Thisbe—Helicon—Thebes—Platæa—Eleutheræ—Athens, 26th March.
Vol. II. *Third Tour*, 17th May 1805. Athens—Phyle—Thebes—*Karditza*—*Martini* — *Andera*— *Talando* (*Atalante*)— Thermopylæ — Lamia — *Styllda* — *Armyró* — *Volo* — *Velestino* — Larissa — Tempe — Pharsalia — *Domokó* (Thaumaci)—Lamia—Thermopylæ—*Dadi*—*Velitza*—Elateia—Orchomenos—Haliartos—Thebes—Delium—Oropos—Marathon—Pentele—Athens, 22d June.
Fourth Tour, 28th November 1805. Athens—Eleusis—Megara—Corinth — Nemea—Argos—Mycenæ—Tiryns—Nauplia —*Ligurio* — Epidaurus — *Damalá* — Trœzen —Calauria — Me-

thana—by *Dara* and *Phanari* to *Piada*—*Hagios Ioannes*—Corinth—*Xylo-kastro*—*Vostitza*—Patrás (with Mr. Gell)—*Palaio-Achaia* — *Mauro-vuna* — *Capelletto* (*Capeleti*) — Elis — *Pyrgo*—Olympia—*Miráka* —*Samikón*—the Neda—Cyparissiæ—*Kleisoura*—*Constantino*—Messene—*Karitena*—Bassæ (where Mr. Gell leaves him)—Lykosoura— *Leondári*—*Mistra*—Sparta—Amyclæ—Tegea—*Tripolitza*—Mantineia—Orchomenos—Stymphalos—Pheneos—Kleitor—*Megaspélion*—Patrás—*Mesolongi*—Ithaca—*Prévesa*—Corfu, 23d April 1806.

Thirty Views in Greece, 1821, royal folio. *Cyclopian or Pelasgic Remains in Greece and Italy*, 131 drawings, 1834, imperial folio.

Clarke, E. D. [1769-1822], LL.D., Fellow of Jesus College, Cambridge. *Travels in various Countries of Europe, Asia, and Africa.* Part II, Greece, Egypt, and the Holy Land, section 2, 1814; section 3, 4to, London, 1816 (also in 8vo, 1816-24).

> Vol. III, chaps. viii-xviii, Oct. 1801. Alexandria to Cos—Patmos [discovery of the MS of Plato, now in the Bodleian]—Naxos— Paros — Antiparos — Syros — Gyarus — *Zia* (Ceos)— Athens.
> Epidaurus—*Ligurio*—the Hieron—Nauplia—Tiryns—Argos—Mycenæ—Nemea—Sicyon—Corinth—discovery of the site of the Isthmian temenos—Megara—Eleusis—Athens.
> Vol. IV, chaps. i-xiii. Marathon—Brauron—Tanagra—the Euripus—Thebes—Platæa—Leuctra—Helicon—Lebadea—Chæronea—Orchomenus. Lebadea—Delphi—ascent of Parnassus—Tithorea—Elatea—Amphiclea—*Bodonitza*—Thermopylæ—Lamia—Pharsalia—Larissa—Tempe—Thessalonica—Neapolis, and by land to Constantinople (Jan. 1802).

Castellan, A. L., *Lettres sur la Morée et les îles de Cérigo, Hydra, et Zante.* 8vo, Paris, 1808.

Walpole, R., of Trinity College, Cambridge ; *Memoirs relating to European and Asiatic Turkey; edited from manuscript journals.* 4to, London, 1817. Includes Mr. Morritt's 'Journey through the District of Maina' in 1795 ; Mr. Raikes's Journey through parts of Bœotia and Phocis (with the discovery of the Corycian cave) ; Mr. Hawkins on the Topography of Athens and the Vale of Tempe ; and papers by Dr. Sibthorp on the Flora and Fauna of Greece. *Travels in Various*

Countries in the East, being a continuation of the above Memoirs, edited 1820.

Gell, W. [1777-1836], Fellow of Emmanuel College, Cambridge. *Narrative of a Journey in the Morea*, 1823, 8vo.

> 1804-5. *Navarino* (excursion to Modon)—*Gargaliáno*—*Philiatrá*—Cyparissia—*Siderokastro*—*Páulitza*—*Tragoge* (excursion to Bassæ)—*Andrítzena*—*Karítena*—*Tripolitza*—Megalopolis—*Leondári*—*Kalamata* (excursion in the *Maina*)—back to *Leondári*—*Mistra*—Sparta—*Tripolitza*—Mantinea—Orchomenos—*Ghiósa* (= *Gíóza*, Caryæ)—Pheneos—Stymphalos—Phlius—*Hagios Georgios*—Argos—Mycenæ—Nemea—Tiryns—Nauplia—*Lygourio* (and Hierum)—Epidaurus—*Damalá*—to Trœzen and Hermione and back, and across to Athens.

The Itinerary of Greece, with a commentary on Pausanias and Strabo, and an account of the monuments of antiquity at present existing in that country, compiled in the years 1801, 1802, 1805, and 1806. [Contains an elaborate Itinerary of Argolis alone]. 4to, London (T. Payne), 1810.

Itinerary of the Morea, being a description of the routes of that peninsula, 12mo, London (Rodwell), 1817; ed. 2, 1827.

Itinerary of Greece, containing one hundred routes in Attica, Bœotia, Phocis, Locris, and Thessaly. 12mo, London (Rodwell), 1819.

Leake, W. M.; F.R.S., etc. [1777-1860]. *Travels in the Morea, with a Map and Plans.* 3 vols. 8vo, London (Murray), 1830.*

> Vol. I. *First Tour*. 22d February 1805. Zante to *Gastúni*—*Pyrgo*—Olympia—*Arkadhía* (Cyparissiæ)—*Londdri*—*Tripolitzá*—*Mistrá* and Sparta—Elos—to *Monemvasía* and back—*Marathonísi* (Gythium)—*Skutári*—Cape Matapan and back to *Tzímova*—by *Vitylo* and *Kitriés* to *Kalamáta*—*Andrússa*—Messene—Navarino—*Mothóni*—*Koróni*—by sea to *Kalamáta*. By *Skala* and *Tragói* to *Pávlitza* (Phigaleia).
> Vol. II. Bassæ—*Andrítzena*—*Karítena*—Megalopolis—*Londári*—*Tripolitzá*—*Alonístena*—*Vitina*—*Dhimitzana* (Teuthis)—*Fandri* (Alipheræ)—*Platiand* (Typaneæ)—*Ai Ianni* (Herœa)—by *Vyzitsa, Strézova*, and *Karnési* to *Kalávryta*, and by *Nezerá* to Patras, 30th May.
> Chap. xv. *Second Tour.* 16th February 1806. Patras by

Karavostási (Dyme) and *Kástro Tornese* to *Gastúni*—Psophis—Cleitor—by *Tara* and *Levídhi* to *Tripolitza*—by *Akhladhókambo* to Argos—Tiryns—Nauplia—Mycenæ—Argos—Lerna—*Astró*—Prasiæ—by *Kastánitza* and *Tzitzina* to Sparta and *Mistra.*
Vol. III. By *Perivólia* and *Barbitza* to *Tripolitzá*—Orchomenus—Pheneus—Stymphalus—discovery of the Styx—*Megaspilio*—*Vostitza*—Patras.
Patras — *Vostitza* — by sea to *Xyló-Kastro* — *Trikkala* — by Sicyon to Corinth. Hierum of the Isthmus—Corinth to Nemea —Phlius—Sicyon—*Xyló-Kastro, Kamáres, Mavra Lithária, Akráta, Trupiá* to *Vostitza* and Patras, 28th April.

Peloponnesiaca: a Supplement to Travels in the Morea. 8vo (Rodwell), London, 1846.

Travels in Northern Greece. 4 vols. 8vo (Rodwell), London, 1835.*

Vol. I. *First Journey.* 9th December 1804-16th January 1805. Epirus.
Second Journey. 12th June 1805-16th February 1806. Ætolia, Acarnania, Epirus, Macedonia and Illyria (chaps. iii-viii).
Chap. ix. 12th November. *Ioánnina—Métzovo—Meteora—Trikkala*—Larissa—Pharsalus—*Dhomokó*—Lamia.
Vol. II. Thermopylæ—*Dhadhi*—*Velitza*—Daulis—Panopeus —Chæroncia — *Livadhía* — Orchomenus — Abæ — Atalanta — Ædepsus — Eastern Locris, and back to *Livadhía.* Haliartus —Thebes — Euripus — Anthedon — Lake Copais—*Kardhitza*—Thebes, to Platæa. By Eleutheræ and Eleusis to Athens, 2d January 1806.
28th January 1806. Athens—*Kephisia*—Marathon—Rhamnus —*Grammatikó*, and by *Varvano* and *Kalamos,* to Oropus—Delium — Tanagra — Thebes — Thespiæ — Leuctra — Ascra — Thisbe—Bulis—*Kyriáki*—Helicon—Stiris—Ambrysus—*Dhesfina* —Delphi—Crissa—Cirrha—*Sálona* — *Épakto* (Naupactus), 16th February 1806.
Vol. III. *Third Journey.* 9th September-23d December 1806. Corfu — Leukas—Ithaca—Cephallenia—Cythera—Melos —Paros—Naxos—Delos—Mykonus—Scyrus—Sciathus, etc.—to Mount Athos. Chaps. xxiv-xxviii ; xxx, xxxi. ; Macedonia xxix ; Larissa and Tempe.
Fourth Journey. Vols. III, IV chaps. xxxii-xxxviii. March 1809. Epirus, Acarnania, and Ætolia.
Vol. IV. chaps. xxxix-xlii. 19th November, 1809 - 16th January 1810. *Ioánnina* to *Métzovo, Stagús,* and *Trikkala*—Larissa — Pharsalus — *Armyro*—*Oreós*—*Volo*—Magnesia—Lake Bœbeis — *Velestino*—Pharsalus—*Kardhitza*—*Trikkala*—*Meteora* —*Ioánnina.*

Hobhouse, Sir John Cam [M.P., created a peer in 1851, as Lord Broughton]. *Journey through Albania and other Provinces of Turkey with Lord Byron.* 4to, London, 1812; ed. 2, 2 vols. 4to, 1813; ed. 3, 2 vols. 8vo, 1856. See *Quarterly Review,* x, 175-203.

26th September 1809. *Prévesa* to *Ioánnina—Tepeleni—Prévesa — Mesolónghi —* Patrás *— l'ostitza —* Delphi *—* Thebes *—* by Phyle to Athens, 25th Dec.
5th March 1810. Pirœus to Smyrna (excursion to Ephesus)—Constantinople, 14th May. 14th July, to *Zea* (Ceos), where Byron left for Athens—Patrás—Tripolitza—and after a tour in the Morea—returned in October to Patras and Athens, which he left on 3d June 1811. He returned to Greece in July 1823, stayed for several months at Cephalonia, and died at Mesolonghi 19th April 1824. See ' Byron in Greece,' in Jebb's *Modern Greece.*

Holland, H., M.D., F.R.S. [1788-1873; physician to the Queen, 1852; baronet, 1853]. *Travels in the Ionian Isles, Albania, Thessaly, Macedonia, etc., during the years* 1812 *and* 1813. 4to, London, 1815; 2d ed., 2 vols. 8vo, 1819. Reviewed in the *Quarterly,* xxiii, 325-360; and the *Edinburgh,* xxv, 455-485; and frequently mentioned in the Life of Lord Byron.

Zante—Cephalonia—Ithaca—Santa Maura—*Prévesa—Salagora—Arta—*by Cinque Pozzi (*Pende Pigádhia*) to *Ioánnina.*
*Zagorá—Métzovo—Metéora—Trikkala—*Larissa—Tempe—by *Platamona* and *Katerína* to *Salonica—*islands of *Chilodromi, Sarakino, Skopelos,* Skiathos*—Trikeri—*gulf of *l'olo—Styllda—Zeitun=Zituni* (Lamia)— *Thomoko—*Pharsalia—Larissa.
Lamia—Thermopylæ—up the valley of Bœotian Cephissus—*Sálona—*Delphi—Chæronea—*Livadia—*Helicon—Lake Copais —Thebes—Thespiæ—Leuctra—Platæa—and by Cithæron and Eleusis, to Athens.
Eleusis—Megara—Corinth—Nemea—Mycenæ—Argos—*Tripolitza—Kalávryta—*Patrás—Zante.
*Prévesa—Arta—*by *Suli* and *Paramythia* to *Ioannina. Zitza —Delvinaki—Libochovo—Argyro-Kastro—* Gardiki*— Telepeni— Carbonara—Pollona—Avlona. Telepeni—Ioannina. Prévesa—*Zante.

Galt, John. *Letters from the Levant, containing views of the State of Society, Manners, Opinions, and Commerce in Greece, and several of the principal Islands of the Archipelago.* 8vo, London (Cadell and Davies), 1813.

Hughes, T. S., Fellow of Emmanuel and formerly Fellow of St. John's College, Cambridge. *Travels in Sicily, Greece, and Albania.* 2 vols. 4to, London, 1820, with 15 maps and plates; new ed., 2 vols. 8vo (omitting the large plates), 1830.

> Vol. I. chaps. v-xvii, September 1813. Zante — Patras — *Kalávryta*—Mantinea—*Tripolitza*—Argos—Tiryns—Nauplia—Mycenæ—Nemea—Corinth—Megara—Athens.
> By Phyle to Thebes—*Livadia* (excursion to Lake Copais and Chæronea)—*Aráchova* to Delphi—*Sálona*—*Galaxidi*—*Prévesa Arta*—*Ioánnina* (excursion to Dramisus—*Devitzianá*—*Vareatis*). On pp. 511-532, Dissertations on the Oracles of Dodona and on the site of that of Delphi by Dr. S. Butler, Head Master of Shrewsbury.
> Vol. II. chap. ix. Excursion to *Zitza*—*Tzarovina*—*Delvinaki*—*Libochovo*—*Argyrokastro*—*Tepeleni*—*Berat*—*Klissura*—*Ostanitza*—*Konitza*—*Mavrovuni* and back to *Ioánnina*. *Paramythia*—*Glyky*—*plain of Phanári*—*Suli*—*Luro*—*Camarina*—*Prévesa*—*Parga*—*Paxo*—*Marlera* (a small island north of Corfu)—and thence to Italy, June 1814.

Forbin, *Voyage dans le Levant.* Paris, 1819.

Turner, *Tour in the Levant.* London, 1820.

Williams, H. W. *Travels in Italy, Greece, and the Ionian Islands.* 8vo, Edinburgh (Constable), 1820.

> Vol. II. Corfu—Zante—Cephalonia—Ithaca—Patras—*Vostizza* Delphi—*Livadia*—Thebes—Eleusis—Athens—Corinth—Patras.

Select Views in Greece, with Classical Illustrations. 2 vols. imperial 8vo, London, 1829.

Laurent, P. E. *Recollections of a Classical Tour through various parts of Greece, Turkey, and Italy,* in 1818, 1819. 4to, London (Whittaker), 1821.

> Ceos—Chios—Troad, etc.—Athens—Epidaurus and Argolis—Tripolitza—Sparta—Leondári—Messene—Bassæ—Olympia—Patras—Santa Maura—Corfu.

Stanhope, Col. Leicester. *Greece in* 1822-24. 8vo, London, 1824.

Waddington, G., Fellow of Trinity College, Cambridge. Visit to Greece in 1823-24. London, 1825.

Anon. *The Modern Traveller in Greece,* 2 vols. (vols. xiv to xv), 32mo, contains useful extracts from the works of travellers in Greece up to the date of its publication. London (Duncan), 1826.

Bulwer, H. Lytton, G.C.B., M.P. [the diplomatist; elder brother of the novelist]. *An Autumn in Greece; comprising sketches of the character, customs, and scenery of the country; with a view of its present critical state. In letters addressed to C. B. Sheridan, Esq. To which is subjoined Greece to the close of* 1825, *by a resident with the Greeks, recently arrived.* 8vo, London (J. Ebers), 1826. The author and Mr. J. Hamilton Browne went out as representatives of the "Greek Committee."

> August 1824. Cephalonia—Zante—Olympia—*Hagios Iohannes*—by *Leondari* to *Tripolitza* and Nauplia (and thence to Smyrna, Malta, and Nice).

Anon. *Sketches in Greece and Turkey; with the present condition and future prospects of the Turkish Empire.* (Ridgway), London, 1833.

> 1832. Albania (and Ali Pasha); *Vonitza* (and General Pisa); *Lepanto* (and General Giavella); Corinth; Attica and Epidaurus (George Mavromichaelis); Castle of *Caritena*; Temple of Phigalia; (The Pirates of the Archipelago); (Ipsilanti, Miaulis); Sardis; Constantinople.

Milnes, Richard Monckton [Lord Houghton]. *Memorials of a Tour in some parts of Greece; chiefly poetical.* London (Moxon), 1834.

Burgess, R., B.D., St. John's Coll., Camb. *Greece and the Levant, or Diary of a Summer's Excursion in* 1834. 2 vols., 32mo. London, (Longmans), 1838.

Giffard, E., Pemb. Coll., Oxon. *Ionian Islands, Athens, and Morea.* London (Murray), 1837.

Slade, Sir Adolphus. (1) *Records of Travels in Turkey, Greece,* etc. in 1829-31. 8vo, London, 1832; ed. in 2 vols., 1833; new ed. 1854. (2) *Travels in Turkey, Greece, and Malta* in 1834-36. 2 vols., 8vo, London, 1837.

Fiedler, C. G. *Reise*, 1834-37 (mainly geological). Leipzig, 1840-41.

Von Klenze, L. *Aphoristische Bemerkungen, gesammelt auf seiner Reise in Griechenland.* 6 plans and views folio. 8vo, Berlin, 1838.

Von Farenheid, F. *Reise durch Griechenland* (pp. 60), *Klein-Asien, etc.*, 1841. Königsberg (Hartung), 1875.

Ross, L. [1806-1859]. *Reisen und Reiserouten durch Griechenland*, I. *Reisen im Peloponnes, mit zwei Karten* [Sellasia; Ager Dentheliates], *und mehren Holzschnitten und Inschriften.* Berlin (Reimer), 1841.*

i. Das Heiligthum der Artemis Limnatis und der Ager Dentheliates zwischen Lakonika und Messenien, pp. 1-24.
ii. Phlius und die Umgegend . . . Sikyon . . . Stymphalos, pp. 25-57.
iii. Pallantion, 58-65.
iv. Zur Topographie Arkadiens nebst Theilen von Messenien, Elis und Argolis. (1) Tegea, 66-73. (2) Megalopolis, 74-84. (3) Megalopolis—*Karyotika Kalybia*, 84-94. (4) Das Nedathal, etc., 94-101. (5) Aliphera, etc., 101-109. (6) Das Kladeosthal, etc., 109-120. (7) Mantineia, etc., 121-139.
v. Wege von Argos nach Tegea und Thyreatis. (1) Argos, Kenchreae, Hysiae, 140-148. (2) Temenion, Lerna, 148-152. (3) Genesion, Apobathmi, Pyramia, Elaeus, 152-157.
vi. Weg aus der Thyreatis nach Sparta. (1) Astros, Thyrea, 158-172. (2) Parnon, Wald Skotitas, das Oenusthal, 172-177.
vii. Weg von Tegea nach Sparta. (1) Skiros, *Krya Vrysis*, etc., 178-181. (2) Sellasia, etc., 181-191.

Wanderungen in Griechenland. 8vo, Halle, 1851.*

Vol. I. Eleusis — Thebes — Lebadea — Daulis — *Ardchova* — Delphi — *Sálona* — Kirrha — *Galaxídi* — *Graviá* — Lamia — Thermopylæ — *Talanti* — Lake Copais — Tanagra — Oropos — *Kephisia*—Athens (1834).
Cyclades. Hydra, Spezzia, Nauplia, Tiryns, Argos, Mycenæ, Nemea, Corinth, Megara, Salamis, 1836. Ægina, 1839.
i. *Reisebilder aus dem Peloponnes.* (1) Isthmus of Corinth to Megaspíläon. (2) *Kalavryta* to Olympia. (3) Olympia to Kyparissia. (4) Messene and *Kalamáta*. (5) To Megalopolis, Mantinea, etc. (6) *Achladókampos* to Argos, Mycenæ, Nemea, Acrocorinthus.
ii. Cyclades (1840).

Vol. II. (1) Argolis and Laconia. (2) Eubœa and the Sporades, 1841. Hymettus, 1843. (1) Phyle and Eleusis; (2) Eubœa, Bœotia, and Locris, 1844. Sunium and Marathon; Eubœa and Mount Orthrys; Œta and Parnassus, 1845. Sparta and the northern *Maina*, 1834.

Carnarvon, Third Earl of [1800-1849]. *Reminiscences of Athens and the Morea; Extracts from a journal of Travels in Greece in* 1839; edited by his son. 12mo, London (Murray), 1869.

7th May. Athens — Megara — Corinth — Nemea — Mycenæ — Nauplia — Lerna — *Akladó-kambo* — *Tripolitza* (Mantinea and Tegea)—Megalopolis—*Leondári*—Sparta —.*Mistra* — Gýthium — across Taygetus by *Panizza* to *Liméni—Tzimova, Kita*, and Cape Matapan — *Kalamáta* — *Vourkáno* — Bassæ — *Andrítzena* —*Karitena—Tripolitza*, and back to Athens by Epidaurus.

Mure, W., of Caldwell [1800-1860]. *Journal of a Tour in Greece and the Ionian Islands, with remarks on the recent history, present state, and classical antiquities of those countries.* 2 vols. 12mo, Edinburgh and London (Blackwood), 1842. †

Corfu — Ithaca—*Petalá* — *Katochí* — *Anatolikó* — *Mesolonghi*— *Scala di Sálona* — Delphi — *Aráchova* — Daulia — Chæronea — Orchomenus — Lake Copais — *Livadia* — Haliartus — Thebes — Platæa and (by *Gyptokastro* and *S. Vlasio* to) Athens.

Megara — Corinth — Cleonæ — Nemea — Mycenæ — Tiryns — Heræum—Argos— Nauplia — Lerna — *Tripolitza* (excursion to Mantinea)—*Kryo-vrysi*—Sparta (excursion to *Nerokampo*)—*Leondari*—*Derveni*—Messene — *Constantino* — Bassæ—*Andrítzena*— Alíphera—*Mokritza*—Olympia — *Pyrgo*—*Ali-Tschelebi*— Patras, and thence to Ancona.

Welcker, F. G. [1784-1868]. *Tagebuch einer Griechischen Reise.* 2 vols., 12mo, Berlin (Hertz), 1865.†

Welcker was fifty-eight years of age when he travelled in Greece; and eighty-one when his journal was first printed, under the editorial care of one of his colleagues at Bonn. As it is not supplied with an index or a table of contents, or with titles at the head of the pages, and is not even divided into chapters, I have consulted the convenience of those who desire to use the book by giving the reference to the proper page in each instance.

Vol. I. 26th January-29th March 1842. Athens and Attica, pp. 23-129. Marathon and Sunium, 129-150.

Tour in the Peloponnesus, 30th March, Megara, pp. 160-163. Kinetha, 164. Kromyon, 165. *Kalamáki*, 166. Isthmian temenos, 167 f. Acrocorinthus, 159 f. Kleonae, 172. Nemea, 174 ff. Charváti, 178. Mycenae, 179-185. Heræum, 186 f. Chonika, 188. Argos, 189-192. Akhladó-kampos, 196. Mantinea, 198. Tripolitza, 200. Tegea, 201 f. Kryo-vrysi, 203. Sellasia, 204. Sparta, 206-220 (Amyklæ, 209; Baphio, 210; Xerokampo, 212; Mistra, 213). Leondari, 221. Thuria, 225. Petalídi (Korone), 230-232. Pylos, 233-239. Kyparissia, 243. Messene, 244-259. Megalopolis, 263. Lykosura, 264. Stála, 267. Ampelonäs, 269. Kakoletri (Ira), 270. Phigalia, 272. Temple of Apollo at Bassæ, 276. Andrítsena, 279. Hagios Ioannis, 280. Olympia, 282-284. Lala, 285. Kamúni, 287. Psophis, 290. Sopotó, 293. Klitor, 294. Sudená, 299. Pheneos, 300. Kastania, 304. Stymphalos, 304 ff. Phlius, 308. Hagios Georgios, 310. Argos, 312 f. Mycenæ, 315-318. Heræum, 319 f. Tiryns, 321. Nauplia, 322-326. Hieron, 328 ff. Epidaurus, 333. Ægina, 334-344. 5th May.

Vol. II. 5th-14th May. Athens (Salamis, pp. 12-16).

Tour in Northern Greece, 15th May. Eleusis, Eleutheræ, 21. Platæa, 23 ff. Thebes, 26-30. Leuktra, 32. Thespiæ, 33. Helicon, 34-39. Haliartos, 40. Lebadea, 42-51 (Orchomenos, 44-49). Chæronea, 52-55. Panopeus, 56. Daulis, 58. Ardáchova, 61. Delphi, 63-77 (Krissa and Kirrha, 70-74, 106). Corycian cave, 78, 114. Agoridni (Charadra), 79. Lilaia, 81, 107. Palaiochóri, 82. Lamia, 84. Styllída, 86. Oreós, 88. Kurkula, 91. Achmet-Aga, 92. Chalkis, 95. Aulis, 97, 105. Tanagra, 99, 107. Skala (Oropos), 101. Markópulo, 102. Dekelea, 103. By Patissia to Athens, 104 (memoranda on Nauplia, Tiryns, Argos, &c., 107-114). 30th May.

30th May-8th June. Athens, pp. 114-129.

Tour in Asia Minor. (Syra, 130.) Smyrna, 134-141. Sidiköe, 142. Metropolis, 145. Agasoluk, 147. Ephesus, 148-153. Magnesia on the Mæander, 154 f. Tralles, 157. Tyra, 160 f. Nymphi, 167. Kassaba, 171. Achmet-loe, 172. Sardes, 173-182. Thyatira, 183 f. Pergamos, 190-199. Assos, 200-205. Aïwadschik, 206. Eski Stambul (Alexandria Troas), 207-212. Ine, 212. Bunarbaschi, 214 ff. Iiaurköi, 223. Rhöteion, 225. Dardanelles, 227. Constantinople, 228-244. Smyrna, 246-256. Syra, 258-264. Mykonos, 265 ff. Delos, 269-277. Tinos, 277. Andros, 279 ff. Karystos, 282 ff. Ocha, 287. Porto Raphti, 290. Athens, 292. 6th August to Kalamáki and Corinth, 296 f. Sikyon, 299-304. Pheneos, 307 ff. Sarugla, 313. Solos, 314. Styx, 316. Kaláryta, 318. Megaspíläon, 319. Vostitza, 321-325. Patras, 326. Korfu, 327. Departure for Ancona, 16th August, 329.

Le Bas, P., and **Waddington**, W. H. *Voyage Archéologique en Grèce et Asie Mineure.* Paris, 1843-73 (mainly on inscriptions).

Stephani, L. *Reisen durch einige Gegenden des nordlichen Griechenlandes.* Leipzig, 1843.

De Vere, Sir Aubrey. *Sketches of Greece and Turkey.* 1850.

Patterson, J. L. *Journal of a Tour in Egypt, Palestine, Syria, and Greece.* 8vo, London, 1852.

Hettner, H. *Athens and the Peloponnesus, with sketches of Northern Greece.* Vol. II of Constable's Miscellany of Foreign Literature. Edinburgh, 1854. Trans. from *Griechische Reiseskizzen*, Braunschweig, 1853.

> April 1852. Athens, pp. 1-125. (With Goettling and Preller) to Eleusis, Megara, Corinth, Nemea, Mycenæ, Argos, Tiryns, Nauplia. By *Tripolitza* and Megalopolis to Messene, Bassæ, Olympia; by *Kaldvryta* to *Megaspilæon*. Athens to Marathon and Thebes, Lebadea, Delphi, Chæronea.

Vischer, W. *Erinnerungen und Eindrücke aus Griechenland.* Basel, 1856-57, 2d ed., pp. 701, 1875.

> 19th March 1853. Corfu—by Cape Matapan to Athens. Sunium, Marathon, Rhamnus; Phyle; Eleusis.
> *Tour in Peloponnesus,* 11th April. Athens to Megara—Corinth —Sicyon—Phlius—Nemea—Cleonæ—Argos—Tiryns—Nauplia —Mycenæ—the Heræum — Argos — *Achladókambos* — *Tripiana* (Nestane)—Mantinea — *Tripolitza* — Tegea—Khan of *Krevatá* (Sellasia)—Sparta—*Leondári*—Megalopolis—*Kokla* (Ampheia?) —Thuria—*Kalamáta*—*Navarino*—*Lygodista*—Messene — Bassæ —*Andrítzena*—Olympia—*Kumáni* — Psophis— Kleitor—*Kaldvryta* — *Megaspélion* — Styx — Pheneos — Stymphalos —Phlius— *Charváti*—Nauplia—the Hieron—Epidaurus—Ægina—Athens, 13th May (32 days).
> *Tour in Northern Greece,* 18th May 1853. Athens by Eleutheræ to Platæa — Leuctra — Thespiæ — Helicon — Haliartus — Onchestus—Thebes—*Karditza*— *Topólia*—Orchomenos—*Livadia* Chæronea—Panopeus and Daulis—to *Distomo* (Ambrysos) and Stiris, and back; by the Schiste to *Aráchova*—Delphi—Krisa— *Sálona*—*Gravia*—*Dadí*—*Velitza* (Tithorea)—*Drachmani* (near Elatea)—*Belesi* (Parapotamioi)—ruins of Abæ and Hyampolis— *Hagios Konstantinos* — Thermopylæ — Lamia — *Andinitza* — *Stylída*—*Lithada*—*Roviés* (Orobiæ)—*Achmet-Aga*—Chalkis— Aulis—Oropus, and by *Kakosialesi* and Phyle to Athens (23 days).

Ussing, J. L. *Griechische Reisen und Studien.* 8vo. Copenhagen, 1857.

Clark, W. G. [1822-1879]; Fellow and Tutor of Trinity College, Cambridge; Public Orator, 1857-69. *Peloponnesus; Notes of Study and Travel.* London (Parker), 1858, 8vo. *

> 1856, with W. H. Thompson, Regius Professor of Greek, 1853-67; Master of Trinity, 1867-86. Athens—Megara—the Isthmus—Corinth—Nemea—Mycenæ—Tiryns—Argos—Karya—*Tzipiana*—Mantinea—*Tripolitza*—Tegea—*Krya Vrysis*—Sparta (excursion to *Xerócampo*)—by *Kastania, Tzernitsa,* and *Ladú* to *Kalamáta*—by *Nisi* and across the *Vélika* to *Navarino*—convent of *Vourkáno* and ruins of Messene—*Paulitza*—Bassæ—*Andritzena* — Olympia — *Pyrgos* — *Ali-Tchelebi* — *Patras* — *Vostizza*—*Megaspelion*—Styx—Pheneos—Stymphalos—*Khaliani*—Sicyon—Corinth.

Senior, W. N. [1790-1864; Professor of Political Economy at Oxford.] *A Journal kept in Turkey and Greece in the autumn of 1857 and the beginning of 1858.* Post 8vo, London, 1859.

> The reviewer in the *Athenæum*, 1859, i 773, says of this journal:—'We hold that the method of it is false and the material collected worthless;' while the *Saturday Review* in the same year describes it as—' By very much the most interesting and instructive book of travels that has come under our notice for a long time.'

Wyse, Sir Thomas, K.C.B., British Minister at Athens, 1849-62. *An Excursion in the Peloponnesus in the year 1858.* 2 vols., London, 1865.

> 7th May 1858. Athens; by sea from Peiræus to Monemvasia, and round Cape Malea to Skutári and Gythium—Sparta and *Mistra*—by *Trype* through the *Langada* pass to *Lada, Koútsova,* and *Kalamáta*—by Thuria to Messene—Eira—Phigaleia—Bassæ —Andrítzena—by Heræa (*Agia-janni*) to Olympia—by Lala and Psophis to *Kaláwryta*—*Megaspélion*—*Vostitza*—along the Achaian coast to Sicyon and Corinth—across the Isthmus to *Kalamáki;* and by sea to the Peiræus, 29th May.

Impressions of Greece (with three letters from Dean Stanley). London (Hurst and Blackett), 1871.

> i. 7th-20th October. *Excursion to Thebes.* Pentelicus—Marathon—Rhamnus—*Sykaminò*—Tanagra — Thebes — Thisbe and Helicon—*Livadia*—Stiris—Chæronea—Orchomenus and Petra —Haliartus—Thebes—by Platæa and Eleutheræ to Athens.
> ii. 1st-11th June. *Excursion in Eubœa.* By steamer from

Peiræus, round Sunium to Chalcis—*Vatonda—Achmet-aga* and *Mandoudi—Kastaniotissa—Oreós—Xerochóri—Bouta—Mandianiká—Achmet-aga*—Chalcis, and back to the Peiræus.
    iii. 4th-9th October. *Excursion to Delphi* (with Dean Stanley). Athens by Platæa to Thebes—by Haliartus to Livadia—Chæronea, Panopeus, and Daulis—to the convent of Jerusalem—Aráchova to the *Kalyvia*—ascent of Parnassus and descent to Delphi and Crissa—Patras.

Tozer, H. F. *Researches in the Highlands of Turkey;* chaps. xx-xxv, on Thessaly. 2 vols. 8vo, London (Murray), 1869.

Symonds, J. A. *Athens,* pp. 207-233, in 'Sketches in Italy and Greece.' Crown 8vo, London (Smith and Elder), 1874.

Breton, E. *Athènes; Voyage dans le Péloponnèse,* ed. 2, 1868.

Rodwell, G. F. *South by East;* chap. xi on Athens, 1877.

Mahaffy, J. P., Professor of Ancient History in the University of Dublin. *Rambles and Studies in Greece* [Athens and Attica ; Thebes and Bœotia ; Delphi ; Argolis ; with 10 illustrations]. Post 8vo, London (Macmillan), 1876 ; ed. 3, revised with an additional chapter on Sparta, 1887. [Chapters on Olympia and Bassæ had already been added in ed. 2.] †

Freeman, E. A. *First Impressions of Athens,* May 1877 ; pp. 278-302 of 'Historical Essays,' Third Series, 8vo, London (Macmillan), 1879.

Jebb, R. C., Professor of Greek in the University of Glasgow. *Modern Greece :* Two Lectures delivered before the Philosophical Institution of Edinburgh [i. ' The Greek nation from the time of Alexander the Great to our own ;' ii. ' Impressions derived from a Recent Visit to Greece,' May 1878 ; Delos, Athens, Delphi, Corinth, Mycenæ, Sparta, Messene, and Olympia, pp. 62-107] ; with Papers on ' The Progress of Greece ' and ' Byron in Greece.' Post 8vo, London (Macmillan), 1880. †

Farrer, R. R. *A Tour in Greece,* 1880. With 27 Illus-

trations by Lord Windsor. Large 8vo, Edinburgh (Blackwood), 1882.
> Corfu — Athens — Thebes — Chalcis — Platæa — Thespiæ — *Livadia* — Delphi—Argolis— *Tripolitza*—*Karytena*—*Andrítzena* Bassæ—Olympia—Zante—Corfu.

Belle, H., premier secrétaire d'ambassade. *Voyage en Grèce* [*Trois Années en Grèce*], *ouvrage contenant* 32 *gravures sur bois et une carte*. Post 8vo, Paris (Hachette), 1881. †
> Tour in *Northern Greece*, pp. 44-218. October 1878? Athens—Eleusis—Thebes—Chalcis—*Achmed-Aga*—*Mantoudi*—*Hagia-Anna*—*Oreos*—*Stylida*—Lamia—Thermopylæ—Daulis—Chæronea—Lake Copais—Orchomenos—*Li:adia*—*Ardkhova*—ascent of Parnassus—Delphi—Krissa—*Sálona*—*Scala di Sálona*—*Vostitza*—Patras—Zante—Corfu.
> Tour in the *Peloponnesus*, pp. 241-408. 10th April 1879 (?). Athens — Megara — *Kalamáki* — Acrocorinthus — Nemea — Mycenæ—Nauplia — *Myli* — Argos — *Palæo-Moukhli* — *Tripolitza*—Tegea—Sparta—*Trypi*, and by the *Languda* over Taygetus to *Lada-Koútsova*—ten days in the *Maina* district—*Kalamáta*—*Navarino*—*Androussa*—*Vourkáno*—Messene—*Karýtena*—valley of the Neda—Bassæ—*Andrítzena*—Olympia—*Kaldvryta*—*Megaspílion*—*Vostitza*—Athens.

Smith, Agnes. *Glimpses of Greek Life and Scenery*. Demy 8vo, London (Hurst and Blackett), 1884.
> 12th April—23d May 1883. A Tour by three ladies; from Athens to Corinth, Argos, *Tripolitza*, Sparta, *Leondari*, Messene, *Andrítzena*, Olympia, *Kalavryta*, *Vostitza*, Delphi, Thebes, Athens.

Krumbacher. *Griechische Reise*, 1886.

Fitz-Patrick, T. *Autumn Cruise in the Ægean*. London (Sampson Low), 1887.

GREEK GEOGRAPHY AND TOPOGRAPHY.
GENERAL.

Strabo [about 60 B.C.-21 A.D.]; books viii-x; ed. Meineke, 3 vols., post 8vo, Leipzig (Teubner), 1852.

Geographi Græci Minores, ed. Carl Müller, 2 vols. royal 8vo, Paris (Didot), 1855-61. Atlas, 1855.

Cramer, J. A. *A Geographical and Historical Description of Ancient Greece* [useful for its quotations from Greek poets and modern travellers]. 3 vols. 8vo. Oxford, 1828.

Stanley, A. P. "Greek Topography," in the *Classical Museum* for 1844, vol. i, pp. 41-81.

Wordsworth, Chr. *Greece: a Descriptive, Historical, and Pictorial Account.* Royal 8vo (Murray), 1839; ed. 2, 1859; revised edition by H. F. Tozer, 1882.

Smith, W. Dictionary of Greek and Roman Geography. 2 vols. (Murray), 1854-57.*

Expédition Scientifique de Morée, 4 vols. 4to (Paris), 1832-36; 3 vols. folio, 1831-38; and folio 'Atlas,' including the Map of the French Survey, and many fine plates.*

Curtius, E. *Peloponnesos; eine historisch geographische Beschreibung* der Halbinsel. 2 vols., 8vo, Gotha (Perthes), 1851-52.*—Do., *History of Greece*, transl. Ward, chap. i.

Bursian, C. *Geographie von Griechenland.* 8vo, Leipzig (Teubner). Vol. i, Northern Greece, 1862; vol. ii, Peloponnesus, and the Islands of Modern Greece and Crete, 1868-72.*

Tozer, H. F. *Lectures on the Geography of Greece.* Small 8vo, London (Murray), 1873.†

SPECIAL.

Athens and Attica.

Stuart and Revett. *The Antiquities of Athens.* 4 vols. folio, 1762, 1789, 1794, London, 1816. New edition, 1825-30.*

Unedited Antiquities of Attica [architectural remains of Eleusis, Rhamnus, Sunium, Thoricus], by the Society of Dilettanti. Folio, London, 1817; ed. 2, 1833.

Leake, W. M., *The Topography of Athens.* 8vo, London

1821 ; ed. 2, as first volume of *Athens and the Demi of Attica*, 1841.*

Wordsworth, Chr., *Athens and Attica.* Post 8vo, London (Murray), 1836 ; ed. 4, 1869. †

Forchhammer, P. W., *Topographie von Athen.* Kiel, 1841.

Penrose, F. C., *Principles of Athenian Architecture.* Folio, London, 1851.

De Laborde, *Athènes aux xv, xvi, et xvii Siècles.* Paris, 1854.

Ross, L., *Archäologische Aufsätze.* Leipzig (Teubner), 1855-61.

Curtius, E., *Attische Studien;* i, Pnyx und Stadtmauer ; ii, Kerameikos und die Geschichte der Agora von Athen. Gotha (Perthes), 1862-65.

Lenormant, F. *La voie sacrée Eleusinienne.* Paris, 1864.

Dyer, T. H. *Ancient Athens, its History, Topography, and Remains.* Large 8vo, London (Bell), 1873.

Wachsmuth, C. *Die Stadt Athen im Alterthum*, vol. i., 8vo. Leipzig (Teubner), 1874.

Milchhöfer, A. Article on "Athens" in Baumeister's *Denkmäler*, Munich, 1885. *Die Attischen Demen*, Berlin, 1887.

Ross, L. *Die Demen von Attika u. ihre Vertheilung unter die Phylen.* 4to, Halle, 1846.

Hanriot. *Recherches sur la topographie des Dèmes de l'Attique.* Paris, 1853.

Ἐφημερὶς ἀρχαιολογική. Quarterly, 4to, Athens.

Mittheilungen des Deutschen Archäologischen Institutes in Athen, 8vo. The quarterly journal of the Athenian branch of the German Archæological Institute. From 1876. Athens.

Bulletin de Correspondance Hellénique; memoirs of the

École Française at Athens; 8vo. eight nos. annually. From 1877. Athens.

Papers of the American School of Classical Studies at Athens, 1882-83, vol. i, large 8vo, Boston, 1885.

THE ACROPOLIS.

Jahn and **Michaelis**, *Pausaniæ descriptio arcis Athenarum*. Small 4to, Bonn (Marcus), 1880.†

Beulé, *l'Acropole d'Athènes*, ed. 2, Paris, 1860.

Burnouf, E., *la Ville et l'Acropole d'Athènes aux diverses époques*, 21 plates, 8vo, Paris, 1877.

THE TEMPLE OF NIKE APTEROS.

Ross, Schaubert, and Hansen. Folio, 13 plates, Berlin, 1839. **R. Kekule**, *Die Balustrade des Tempels*. 3 plates, 8vo, Leipzig, 1869. *Die Reliefs*. 7 plates, plans, and woodcuts, folio, Stuttgart, 1881.

THE PROPYLÆA.

Bohn, R. *Die Propyläen der Akropolis, aufgenommen u. dargestellt.* Folio, 21 plates in portfolio, Stuttgart, 1883.

THE PARTHENON.

Bröndsted, P. O. *Voyage de la Grèce*, vol. ii. Large 4to, Paris (Didot), 1826.

Michaelis, A., *Der Parthenon*. Royal 8vo, with atlas of 15 plates, imp. folio, Leipzig, 1871.*

THE ERECHTHEUM.

Inwood, H. W. Folio, London, 1827.—**Quast, A. F.** Folio, 42 plates, Berlin, 1843. — **Forchhammer, P. W.** 2 plates, 4to, Kiel, 1879.

Fowler, H. N., in *Papers of the American School*, vol. i, pp. 213-236.

Tétaz, *Revue Archéologique*, 1851.

Fergusson, J., and A. S. Murray, *Journal of Hellenic Studies*, vol. i-ii.

THEATRE OF DIONYSUS.

Vischer, W., *Kleine Schriften*, ii, pp. 324-390.

Julius, L., in *Zeitschrift für bildende Kunst*, vol. xiii, 1877.

Wheeler, J. R., in *Papers of the American School*, vol. i, pp. 123-179.

Müller, A., *Die Griechischen Bühnenalterthümer*, pp. 432. Large 8vo, Freiburg (I.B.), 1886.

THE ASCLEPIEION.

Girard, P. 8vo, maps and 3 plates; 8vo, Paris, 1881.

THE OLYMPIEION.

Beier, L., in *Papers of the American School*, vol. i, pp. 181-212.

THE PANATHENAIC STADIUM.

Ziller, E., *Ausgrabungen*. 4 plates, 4to, Berlin, 1870.

THE PNYX.

Welcker, G. F. (1) In *Tagebuch*, ii 116-118. (2) *Der Felsaltar des Höchsten Zeus oder das Pelasgikon in Athen, bisher genannt die Pnyx. Nach der Entdeckung des Prof. H. N. Ulrichs in Athen.* Acad. der Wissenschaften, Berlin, 1852, pp. 267-336. — Ulrichs, H. N., *Reisen u. Forschungen*, ii, 209-212.—Curtius, E. *Attische Studien*, i, 1862; and *Erläuternder Text* to *Sieben Karten*, pp. 16-18. Gotha, 1868.

Ross, L., *Die Pnyx u. das Pelasgikon in Athen.* 3 plates, 8vo, Braunschweig, 1853.

Bursian, C., in the *Philologus*, ix, p. 631.—Rangabé, *Antiquités Helléniques*, vol. ii, 579-586. 4to, Athens, 1855. Dyer's *Athens*, pp. 531-542.

THE THESEUM.

Ross, L. τὸ Θησεῖον καὶ ὁ ναὸς τοῦ "Αρεως. Athens, 1838. Do., revised and enlarged in *Das Theseion*, Halle, 1852.

THE STOA OF ATTALUS II.

Adler, F. Folio, 7 plates, 1875.—**Bohn, R.** Folio, 2 plates, Berlin, 1882.

THE MUSEUMS.

Milchhöfer, A. *Die Museen Athens.* Athens, 1881.

Von Sybel, L. *Katalog der Sculpturen zu Athen.* Athens, 1881.

Heydemann, H. *Die Antiken Marmor-Bildwerke zu Athen.* Berlin, 1874.

Collignon, Max. *Catalogue des Vases peints du Musée de la Société Archéologique d'Athènes.* · Paris, 1878.—
J. Martha, Do., *De figurines en terres cuites.* 8 plates, 8vo, Paris, 1880.

Bœotia.

Ulrichs, H. N. *Reisen u. Forschungen*, part ii. 8vo, Berlin (Weidmann), 1863.

Stanhope, J. S. *Topography of the battle of Platæa.* Atlas, London, 1817.

Eubœa.

Ulrichs (*l.c.*); and other authorities mentioned in Bursian's *Geogr.* ii, 395 *n.*

Delphi.

Ulrichs, H. N. *Reise über Delphi* (pp. 1-157), *durch Phocis u. Boeotien bis Theben. In Reisen u. Forschungen*, part i. 8vo, Bremen (Heyse), 1840.

Curtius, E. *Anecdota Delphica.* 4to, Berlin (Besser), 1843.

P. Foucart and C. Wescher. *Inscriptions recueillies à Delphes.* 8vo, Paris, 1863.—Foucart. *Mémoire sur les ruines et l'histoire de Delphes.* 8vo, Paris, 1865.

Mommsen, A. *Delphica.* Leipzig, 1877.

Haussoullier, B, in *Bulletin de Correspondance Hellénique,* 1881-1882.

Ætolia.

Bazin. *Archives des Missions,* 2e serie, t. i.

Acarnania.

Heuzey. [*Le Mont Olympe et*] *l'Acarnanie.* Paris (Didot), 1860.

Thessaly.

Kriegk. *Das thessalische Tempe.* Leipzig, 1835. *Die thessalische Ebene.* Frankfort, 1858.

Mezières, A. *Le Pelion et l'Ossa.* Paris, 1853.

Ægina.

About, E. *Archives des Missions,* 1re serie, t. iii. Garnier, *Revue de l'Orient,* mai 1857; *Revue Archéologique,* 1854.

Cockerell, C. R., and W. W. Lloyd. *The Temple of Jupiter Panhellenius, etc.* Folio, London, 1860.

Argolis.

Schliemann, H. *Mycenæ,* 1878. *Tiryns,* 1886. Royal 8vo, London (Murray).

Newton, C. T., on Dr. Schliemann's Discoveries at Mycenæ, in *Essays on Art and Archæology,* pp. 246-302. London (Macmillan), 1880.

Sparta.

Dressell and **Milchhöfer**, Catalogue of the Museum of Antiquities, in Mitth. Deutschen Arch. Inst., vol. ii, pp. 293-474.

Arcadia.

Schwab, C. T. *Arcadien, seine Natur, seine Geschichte, seine Einwohner, seine Alterthümer;* a pamphlet. Tübingen, 1852.

De la Coulonche. *Archives des Missions,* 1re serie, t. vii, p. 204.

Rangabé, A. *Mémoires de l'Académie des Inscriptions,* t. v. Paris.

Sparta, Arcadia, Elis, Achaia.

Beulé, E. *Études sur le Péloponnese.* Paris (Didot), 1855, 1875.

Triphylia.

Boutan. *Archives de Missions Scientifiques,* 2e serie, t. i, pp. 193-248. Paris.

Olympia.

Curtius, Adler, Hirschfeld. *Die Ausgrabungen von Olympia.* 5 vols., square folio, with numerous photographs, Berlin, 1827-1881.*

Die Funde von Olympia. 40 plates in portfolio, Berlin, 1882.

Boetticher, A. *Olympia, das Fest und seine Stätte.* Large 8vo, Berlin, 1883. 2d ed. 1885.

Förster, B. *Ein Blick auf den allgemeinen Kunst- und kulturhistorischen Werth der Grabungen am Alpheios, mit vier Abbildungen,* pp. 25. Halle (Hendel), 1886.

Newton, C. T. *Essays on Art and Archæology,* pp.

321-372. Discoveries at Olympia. London (Macmillan), 1880.

Flach. Article on *Olympia* in Baumeister's *Denkmäler*, 1886-1887.

Bassæ.

Von **Stackelberg**, O. M. *Der Apollotempel zu Bassæ in Arkadien u. die daselbst ausgegrabenen Bildwerke.* Folio, 31 plates; Rome, 1826. — *O. M. von Stackelberg; Schilderung seines Lebens u. seiner Reisen, nach Tagebüchern u. Briefen;* by his niece, N. de Stackelberg.

Cockerell, C. R., and W. W. **Lloyd.** *The Temples of [Jupiter Panhellenius and] Apollo Epicurius.* Folio, London, 1860.

THE IONIAN ISLANDS.

Goodisson, W. *An Historical and Topographical Essay upon the Islands of Corfu, Leucadia, Ithaca, Cephalonia and Zante.* 8vo, London, 1822. — **Liebtrut**, F. *Reise nach den Ionischen Inseln, Korfu, Zante, Cephalonia, Ithaka.* Hamburg, 1850. — **Ansted.** *The Ionian Islands in the year* 1863. London, 1863. —**Riemann.** *Recherches Archéologiques sur les Iles Ioniennes.* Paris, 1879-1880.

Mystoxidi, A. *Illustrazioni Corciresi.* 2 vols., Milan, 1811-1814; and *Delle cose Corciresi*, vol. i, Corfu, 1848. [On the author, see Welcker's *Tagebuch*, ii, 327.] **Gregorovius**, *Corfu, eine Ionische Idylle.* Leipzig, 1882.

Warsberg, *Odysseeische Landschaften.* 2 vols., Vienna, 1878.—**Stillman**, W. J. "On the Track of Ulysses;" articles in the *Century Magazine*, May–October, 1884, pp. 562, 688, 882.

Gell, W. *The Geography and Antiquities of Ithaca*, 4to, London, 1807.—**Bowen**, G. F. *Ithaca in* 1850. A pamphlet. London, ed. 3, 1854.

THE GREEK ISLANDS OF THE ÆGEAN.

Randolph, B. *The Present State of the Islands of the Archipelago.* Oxford, 1687.

Dapper, O. *Description des Iles de l'Archipel.* Folio, Amsterdam, 1703.

De Tournefort, P. *Voyage du Levant.* 3 vols. 8vo, Paris, 1717.

Choiseul-Gouffler, Comte de. *Voyage Pittoresque de la Grèce.* 3 vols. folio, Paris, 1782.

Bröndsted, P. O. *Voyage dans la Grèce.* Vol. i contains full description, topographical and archæological, of the island of Keos. 4to, Paris (Didot), 1826.

Ross, L. *Reisen auf den Griechischen Inseln des Agäischen Meeres.* 4 vols. 8vo, Stuttgart and Tübingen, 1840-1852.

Tozer, H. F. (1) "Notes of a Tour in the Cyclades and Crete," published in *The Academy*, 1875. (2) "In the Asiatic Greek Islands"—Lesbos, Chios, Samos, Patmos, Rhodes—in *The Academy*, 21st August to 16th October 1886.

Bent, J. T. *The Cyclades; or, Life among the Insular Greeks.* Crown 8vo, London (Longmans), 1885.

Delos: J. A. **Lebégue**, *Recherches sur Delos*, Paris, 1876. Th. **Homolle**, *Monuments Grecs*, No. 7, 1878, and *Bulletin de Correspondance Hellenique*, vols. i-x, 1877-86. R. C. **Jebb**, *Journal of Hellenic Studies*, pp. 7-62, 1880.

GUIDE-BOOKS.

Murray's Handbook for Travellers in Greece, including the Ionian Islands, Continental Greece, the Peloponnese, the Islands of the Ægean, Crete, Albania, Thessaly, and Macedonia. Post 8vo, with maps and plans, ed. 5, in two parts, pp. 741, London, 1884, 24s. †

GUIDE-BOOKS AND MAPS

Guide Joanne; Grèce et Turquie d'Europe, par Dr. E. Isambert; ed. 3 in preparation. Post 8vo, Paris (Hachette).

Baedeker's Griechenland, mit einem Panorama von Athen, 6 Karten, 7 Plänen und andern Beigaben. Leipzig, 1883. 7s. 6d.†

Meyer's Palästina, Griechenland [pp. 203-376], *u. Türkei*, mit 8 Karten, 20 Plänen, etc. Leipzig, 1882. 12s. 6d.

Reinach, S. *Conseils aux Voyageurs Archéologues en Grèce et dans l'Orient Hellenique.* Paris (Leroux), 1886. †

ATLASES, MAPS, AND PLANS.

(The prices are those at which the maps are supplied by Stanford, Charing Cross.)

Smith, W. *Historical Atlas of Ancient Geography*, by C. Müller and G. Grove. 126s. London (Murray), 1873-76.

Kiepert, H. *Atlas von Hellas und den hellenischen Colonien.* 15 maps, imp. folio, 26s. Berlin, 1871.

Spruner-Menke. *Atlas Antiquus* (31 maps), with descriptive text, folio, 35s. Gotha, 1865.

The English Admiralty Charts are the best for the Ionian Islands and the Archipelago, and for the Coasts of Greece. For detailed lists and prices see pp. 37-39 of the *Catalogue of Admiralty Charts*, 1885, 1s.; sold by Stanford, Charing Cross.

French Survey, *Map of Modern Greece* (exclusive of the Ionian Islands). 20 sheets, executed in 1829-31, published in 1832, and also included in the 'Atlas' of the *Expédition Scientifique de la Morée*; reissued in a revised form in 1852. Scale, 1:200,000, or 3.15 miles to an inch; size, 109 inches by 97. Mounted in case, 60s. *

The map in Leake's *Peloponnesiaca* is reduced from the French map on a scale of something more than one-third.

Kiepert's *Map of Modern Greece.* Scale, 1 : 800,000, or 12.62 miles to an inch ; size, 27 inches by 22. Mounted in case, 6s. (Reimer), Berlin. †

This is the most convenient small map of Greece, but the names are not always marked with sufficient distinctness.

Arrowsmith's [or Stanford's London Atlas] *Map of Greece and the Ionian Islands.* Scale, 15 miles to an inch ; size, 22 inches by 26. 3s. ; mounted in case, 5s. The names are clearly marked.

Austrian Staff *Map of Modern Greece.* Scale, 4¾ miles to an inch ; size, 70 inches by 71. 25s. ; mounted in case, 42s.[1] Vienna (Lechner), 1886. †

This is the most recent large map of Greece. It is the joint work of Austrian and Greek surveyors. The railway lines are indicated, and the names are very distinctly marked, though the spelling is not always satisfactory, and the names Attika and Boiotia are accidentally interchanged.

Athens and Attica.

Curtius, E. *Sieben Karten von Athen, mit* * *Text.* Folio, 18s. Gotha, 1868.

Curtius, E., and **J. A. Kaupert.** *Atlas von Athen.* (1), Athens and neighbourhood, on a scale of 1 : 12,500. (2), Ancient Athens, do. (3), S.W. Athens, on a scale of 1 : 4000. (4)-(12), *Felsmonumente,* &c. With explanatory text, folio, 24s. Berlin (Reimer), 1878. (1) and (2) are sold separately at 2s. each, or mounted in case, 3s. 8d. †

Curtius, E., and **J. A. Kaupert.** *Atlas von Attica.* Part i (1881), 4 maps of Athens and the Peiræus, with letterpress, 12s. The first two maps are the same as (1) and (2) in the *Atlas von Athen.* Parts ii-iv (1883-86), 13 sheets of survey of Attica. Scale, 1 : 25,000. Athen-Peiræus, Athen-Hymettos, Kephisia, Pyrgos (from Liossia on the E. to Kalyvia on the W.), Spata, Vari, Raphina, Perati, Porto-Raphti, Pentelikon, Markopulo, Cap Sunion (2 sheets). Berlin (Reimer).

---

[1] Sold in sheets by Deighton and Bell, Cambridge, for 17s., or 1s. 6d. per sheet.

Burn, R. *Relief Map of Athens and the Peiraieus*, modelled by H. F. Brion, 22 Philip Road, Peckham Rye, London, 1881.

Michaelis, A. *Plan der Akropolis.* 16s. Cassel, Fischer, 1876.

Mycenæ.

Steffen, *Karten von Mykenai.* Two maps; with a sketch map of Argolis and an appendix, by H. Lolling, on the mountain district between Mycenæ and Corinth. 12s. Berlin (Reimer), 1884.†

Olympia.

Stanhope, J. S. *Topography of Olympia*, Atlas, 1824.

Kaupert and Dörpfeld, *Olympia und Umgegend; zwei Karten und ein Situationsplan;* with letterpress by Curtius and Adler. 4s. 8vo, Berlin (Reimer), 1882.†

PHOTOGRAPHS.

Baron Paul des Granges. *Classical Landscapes and Monuments of Greece.* Larger size, 47 cm. by 65 cm., mounted 4s. 6d. each, unmounted 4s. Smaller size, 32 cm. by 45 cm., 2s. 6d. and 2s. 3d. Ed. Quaas, 2 Stechbahn, Berlin.

Constantin. 90 photographs of ancient monuments, landscapes, etc., in Athens and Attica, and in Argolis: in three sizes. (1) $15\frac{3}{4}$ inches by 12, at 3 *fr.*; mounted 4 *fr.* (2) $10\frac{1}{2}$ by $8\frac{1}{4}$, at 1.50 *fr.*; mounted 2 *fr.* (3) $8\frac{1}{4}$ by $6\frac{1}{4}$, at 1 *fr.*; mounted 1.50 *fr.* 3 Rue d'Hermes, Athens.

Stillmann, W. J. *Photographs of Athens.* [Some of the finest photographs in this series are distinguished by an asterisk.] (1)* *Acropolis* and Theseum; (2)* Do. from Museum Hill; (3)* Do. from Stadium Hill; (4)* Do. from the Hill of the Nymphs; (5) Temple of

Wingless Victory; (6) Doorway of Pandrosium; (7) Portico of Do.; (8) *Parthenon*, East Front; (9) Do. from N.E.; (10)* Frieze of the Parthenon (*in situ*); (11) East Portico; (12) West Portico; (13)* *Erechtheum* from Parthenon; (14) Do. West Side; (15) East Side; (16) Interior of cella; (17) Architectural details; (18) Caryatid; (19) Theatre of Herodes Atticus; (20)* *Theatre of Dionysus* (general view of interior); (21)* Do. showing auditorium; (22)* Propylæa, from S.W.; (23) Propylæum and North Wing; (24) Temple and precincts of Asclepius; (25) Old Cathedral of Athens. Uniformly mounted on Cream Boards, 24 by 21, 6s. 6d. each; to Members of the Hellenic Society, 4s. 6d. Autotype Company, 74 New Oxford Street, W.

FLORA.

Sibthorp, J. [1758-1796; Prof. of Botany at the University of Oxford]. *Flora Græca*, edited by J. E. Smith and J. Lindley, in 20 fasciculi, royal folio, with 1000 coloured plates. London, 1807. New ed. 12 vols. folio (Bohn), 1845-46.*

Smith, J. E., M.D., *Floræ Græcæ Prodromus:* "a description of all the known plants belonging to the *Flora Græca*, whether figured therein or not." 2 vols. 8vo, London 1806-13.

Von Heldreich, Th. *Die Nutzpflanzen Griechenlands.* Athens, 1862; and *Die Pflanzen der Attischen Ebene.* Schleswig, 1877 (in A. Mommsen's *Gr. Jahreszeiten*).

Unger, F. *Wissenschaftliche Ergebnisse einer Reise in Griechenland, u. in den Ionischen Inseln.* Vienna (Braumüller), 1862.

MANNERS AND CUSTOMS, FOLK LORE, &c.

Guys, *Voyage Littéraire de la Grèce, ou Lettres sur les Grecs, anciens et modernes, avec un parallel de leurs mœurs.* 2 vols. post 8vo, Paris, 1776; ed. 3, with two more vols., 1783.

Douglas, F. S. N. *An Essay on certain points of resemblance between the ancient and modern Greeks*, pp. 198. 8vo, London (Murray); 3d ed. 1813.

Forchhammer, P. W., *Hellenika, Griechenland im neuen das alte.* 2 maps. 8vo, Berlin, 1837.

Wachsmuth, C. *Das alte Griechenland im neuen. Mit einem Anhang über Sitten und Aberglauben der Neugriechen bei Geburts, Hochzeit u. Tod.* Post 8vo, Bonn (Cohen), 1864.

Schmidt, B. *Das Volksleben der Neugriechen u. das Hellenische Alterthum*, i. Large 8vo, Leipzig (Teubner), 1871; and *Griechische Märchen, Sagen u. Volkslieder, ibid.* 1877.

Von Hahn, J. G. *Griechische u. Albanesische Märchen.* 2 vols, 12mo, Leipzig (Engelmann), 1864.—*Albanesische Studien* [on the topography, archæology, history, manners and customs, folk-lore and language of Albania]. 8vo, Jena, 1854.

Tozer, H. F. *The Highlands of Turkey:* chap. 21, "The Eastern Vampire"; 28, "The Romaic Ballads"; 29, "The Modern Greek Popular Tales"; 30, "Classical Superstitions." London (Murray), 1869.

Ampère, J. J. *La Grèce,* [*Rome et Dante*]. Ed. 6. Paris (Didier), 1870.

Houssaye, H. *Athènes,* [*Rome, Paris*]. *L'histoire et les mœurs.* Ed. 2. Paris (Lévy), 1879.

Δελτίον τῆς ἱστορικῆς ἐθνολογικῆς ἑταιρίας. 8vo; a quarterly journal. Athens.

MODERN GREEK.

Leake, W. M. *Researches in Greece.* 4to, London, 1814.

Mullach, F. W. A. *Grammatik der griechischen Vulgärsprache in historischer Entwicklung.* 8vo, Berlin, 1856.

Contopoulos, N.   Greek-English and English-Greek Lexicon.   2 vols. in 1, 8vo, Athens, 1880.

Legrand, E.   *Dictionnaire Grec moderne-Français.*   18mo, Paris, 1883.

Geldart, E. M.   *The Modern Greek Language in its relation to ancient Greek* [mainly philological].   Extra fcp., 8vo, Oxford, 1870.

Vincent, E., and Dickson, T. G.   *A handbook to Modern Greek* [mainly practical: includes Grammar, Dialogues, passages from Greek authors, Vocabulary, and an Appendix (by Prof. Jebb) "On the relation of Modern to Classical Greek, especially in regard to Syntax"].   Ed. 2, revised and enlarged, crown 8vo, London (Macmillan), 1881.†

APPENDIX II

TIME-TABLES

THE principal *routes to Greece* are :—

(1) *Viâ* **Marseilles**, (a) by the Messageries Maritimes steamers, every Saturday, in five days, going alternately either to Peiræus or Syra. Or (b) *viâ* Marseilles and Genoa, by the Fraissinet steamers, on Thursdays to Peiræus, or on Sundays to Syra.

(2) *Viâ* **Naples**, (a) by the Messageries Maritimes to Peiræus, on alternate Mondays ; or (b) by the Fraissinet steamers, every week.

(3) *Viâ* **Brindisi**, (a) by Hellenic steamer on Fridays by Corfu and Patras to Corinth ; or (b) by Austrian Lloyd on Fridays to Corfu, and thence by Hellenic steamer to Corinth ; or (c) by Florio Rubattino steamer on Thursdays to Corfu, and thence by Panhellenic steamer to Corinth.

(4) *Viâ* **Trieste**, by Austrian Lloyd to Corfu, either on Saturdays (direct), or on Tuesdays, or on alternate Wednesdays.

For further details see the current numbers of the Continental Time-Tables in ordinary use.

GREEK STEAMERS

There are three Companies :—

(1) The HELLENIC ('Ελληνικὴ ἀτμοπλοϊκὴ ἑταιρία). Office, in *Athens*, in the Place de la Concorde (πλατεία τῆς ὁμονοίας), south-west corner, the second house to the right, as you look down Peiræus Street. In *Peiræus*, in the Place d'Apollon, between the Railway Station and the north-east side of the harbour. This Company is often called the *Old Hellenic* to distinguish it from the two others.

(2) The Panhellenic (Πανελλήνιος ἀτμοπλοΐα). Office, in *Athens*, at the Maison Melás, Rue d'Eole, near the 'Theatre' and Banque Nationale. In *Peiræus*, Place d'Apollon.

(3) Gudé and Company ('Ελληνικὴ ἀτμοπλοΐα Δ. Π. Γουδῆ). Office in *Peiræus* only, corner of the Bourse, north-east of the harbour.

Owing to the Greek names of the three Companies resembling one another, it is important to make sure of going to the right office in each case.

1. SYRA—PEIRÆUS—CORINTH

		Hellenic.	Goudé.
Syra (Σύρος)	dep.	Thurs. 7.0 P.M.	...
Peiræus	arr.	Fri. 4.30 A.M.	...
	dep.	Sat. 7.0 ,,	Fri. 7.0 A.M.
Æ'gina	arr.	,, 8.45 ,,	...
	dep.	,, 9.0 ,,	...
Poros	arr.	,, 11.15 ,,	...
	dep.	,, 11.30 ,,	...
Hydra	arr.	,, 12.45 P.M.	Fri. 10.30 A.M.
	dep.	,, 1.0 ,,	,, 11.0 ,,
Spezzia	arr.	,, 2.45 ,,	,, 1.30 P.M.
	dep.	,, 3.0 ,,	,, 1.45 ,,
Cheli(on)	arr.	,, 3.30 ,,	...
	dep.	,, 3.45 ,,	...
· Nauplia	arr.	,, 6.45 ,,	...
	dep.	Sun. 1.45 A.M.	...
Leonídi(on)	arr.	,, 5.0 ,,	Fri. 3.15 P.M.
	dep.	,, 5.15 ,,	,, 3.30 ,,
Kyparissi		Calls in summer.	...
Monemvasía	arr.	Sun. 9.15 A.M.	...
	dep.	,, 9.30 ,,	...
Kýthera	arr.	,, 1.30 P.M.	...
	dep.	,, 1.45 ,,	...
Gýtheion	arr.	,, 6.30 ,,	Fri. 11.0 P.M.
(*Marathonisi*)	dep.	,, 10.30 ,,	,, midnight.
Liméni	arr.	Mon. 4.0 A.M.	...
	dep.	,, 4.15 ,,	...
Kalamáta	arr.	,, 7.15 ,,	Sat. 8.0 A.M.
	dep.	,, 11.0 ,,	,, 10.0 ,,
Nesí		Calls in summer.	...
Koróne	arr.	Mon. 12.45 P.M.	Sat. 11.30 A.M.

SYRA—PEIRÆUS—CORINTH.—*Continued.*

1.		Hellenic.		Goudé.	
Koróne	dep.	Mon.	1.0 P.M.	Sat.	Noon.
Methóne		Calls in summer.		...	
Pylos	arr.	Mon.	5.15 P.M.	Sat.	4.0 P.M.
(*Navarino*)	dep.	Tues.	4.0 A.M.	Sun.	5.0 A.M.
Márathos	arr.	,,	5.15 ,,	,,	6.0 ,,
	dep.	,,	5.30 ,,	,,	7.30 ,,
(H)agía Kyriaké		Calls in		arr.	8.0 ,,
		summer		dep.	9.0 ,,
Kyparissía	arr.	Tues.	7.30 A.M.	,,	10.30 ,,
	dep.	,,	7.45 ,,	,,	11.0 ,,
Katákolo(n)	arr.	,,	11.30 ,,	,,	1.30 P.M.
	dep.	,,	12.30 P.M.	,,	2.0 ,,
Zante	arr.	,,	3.30 ,,	,,	4.30 ,,
	dep.	Wed.	7.0 A.M.	Mon.	8.0 A.M.
Kyllene	arr.	,,	9.15 ,,	,,	9.30 ,,
(*Clarenza*)	dep.	,,	9.30 ,,	,,	10.0 ,,
Mesolongi(on)	arr.	,,	12.30 P.M.	,,	1.30 P.M.
	dep.	,,	1.0 ,,	,,	2.30 ,,
Patras	arr.	,,	3.0 ,,	,,	4.0 ,,
	dep.	Thurs.	9.0 A.M.	,,	9.0 ,,
Náupaktos	arr.	,,	10.15 ,,		...
	dep.	,,	10.30 ,,		...
Æ'gion	arr.	,,	12.15 P.M.	Mon.	11.30 P.M.
(*Vostitza*)	dep.	,,	12.30 ,,	,,	midnight.
Vitrinitsa	arr.	,,	1.45 ,,		...
	dep.	,,	2.0 ,,		...
Galaxídi(on)	arr.	,,	3.30 ,,		...
	dep.	,,	3.45 ,,		...
Itéa	arr.	,,	4.15 ,,		...
	dep.	,,	midnight.		...
Corinth	arr.	Fri.	5.0 A.M.	Tues.	6.0 A.M.

2. CORINTH—PEIRÆUS—SYRA

		Hellenic.			Goudé.		
Corinth	dep.	Wed.	1.0	P.M.	Tues.	Noon.	
Itéa	arr.	,,	6.0	,,	...		
	dep.	,,	6.15	,,	...		
Galaxídi(on)	arr.	,,	6.45	,,	...		
	dep.	Thurs.	4.30	A.M.	...		
Vitrinitsa	arr.	,,	6.0	,,	...		
	dep.	,,	6.15	,,	...		
Æ'gion	arr.	,,	7.30	,,	Tues.	5.0	P.M.
(*Vostitza*)	dep.	,,	7.45	,,	,,	6.0	,,
Náupaktos	arr.	,,	9.30	,,	...		
	dep.	,,	9.45	,,	...		
Patras	arr.	,,	11.0	,,	Tues.	8.30	P.M.
	dep.	,,	12.30	P.M.	Wed.	2.0	A.M.
Mesolongi(on)	arr.	,,	2.30	,,	...		
	dep.	,,	3.0	,,	...		
Kyllene	arr.	,,	6.0	,,	Wed.	6.0	A.M.
(*Clarenza*)	dep.	,,	6.15	,,	,,	6.30	,,
Zante	arr.	,,	8.30	,,	,,	8 [or 7]	,,
	dep.	Fri.	7.0	A.M.	,,	9 [or 8]	,,
Katákolo(n)	arr.	,,	10.0	,,	,,	11.30	,,
	dep.	,,	10.30	,,	,,	Noon.	
Kyparissía	arr.	,,	2.15	P.M.	,,	2.30	P.M.
	dep.	,,	2.30	,,	,,	3.0	,,
(H)agía Kyriaké		...		arr.	,,	4.30	,,
		...		dep.	,,	5.0	,,
Márathos	arr.	Fri.	4.30	,,	,,	6.0	,,
	dep.	,,	4.45	,,	,,	6.30	,,
Pylos	arr.	,,	6.0	,,	,,	7.30	,,
(*Navarino*)	dep.	Sat.	1.15	A.M.	Thurs.	3.0	A.M.
Koróne	arr.	,,	5.30	,,	,,	6.30	,,

CORINTH—PEIRÆUS—SYRA.—*Continued.*

		Hellenic.			Goudé.		
Koróne	dep.	Sat.	5.45	A.M.	Thurs.	7.0	A.M.
Kalamáta	arr.	,,	7.30	,,	,,	8.30	,,
	dep.	,,	10.0	,,	,,	10.0	,,
Liméni	arr.	,,	1.0	P.M.	...		
	dep.	,,	1.15	,,	...		
Gýtheion	arr.	,,	6.45	,,	Thurs.	5.0	P.M.
(*Marathonisi*)	dep.	Sun.	1.0	A.M.	,,	8.0	,,
Kýthera	arr.	,,	5.45	,,	...		
	dep.	,,	6.0	,,	...		
Monemvasía	arr.	,,	10.0	,,	...		
	dep.	,,	10.15	,,	...		
Leonídi(on)	arr.	,,	2.15	P.M.	Fri.	6.0	A.M.
	dep.	,,	2.30	,,	,,	6.15	,,
Nauplia	arr.	,,	5.45	,,	...		
	dep.	Mon.	6.0	A.M.	...		
Cheli(on)	arr.	,,	9.0	,,	...		
	dep.	,,	9.15	,,	...		
Spezzia	arr.	,,	9.45	,,	Fri.	8.0	A.M.
	dep.	,,	10.0	,,	,,	8.30	,,
Hydra	arr.	,,	11.45	,,	,,	10.15	,,
	dep.	,,	Noon.		,,	10.30	,,
Poros	arr.	,,	1.15	P.M.	...		
	dep.	,,	1.30	,,	...		
Æ'gina	arr.	,,	3.45	,,	...		
	dep.	,,	4.0	,,	...		
Peiræus	arr.	,,	5.45	,,	Fri.	2.30	P.M.
	dep.	Tues.	7.0	P.M.	...		
Syra (Σύρος)	arr.	Wed.	4.30	A.M.	...		

3. SYRA—PEIRÆUS—GYTHEION, &c.

		Hellenic.		² Πανελλήνιος.	
Syra [1]	dep.	Mon.	8.0 A.M.	Tues.	8.0 P.M.
Kea (Keos)	arr.	,,	12.30 P.M.	...	
	dep.	,,	1.0 ,,	...	
Láurion		Calls.		...	
Peiræus	arr.	,,	6.15 ,,	Wed.	5.30 A.M.
	dep.	Tues.	10.0 A.M.	Thurs.	7.0 ,,
Gýtheion	arr.	Wed.	1.0 ,,	,,	9.45 P.M.
	dep.	,,	3.0 ,,	,,	midnight.
Kalamáta	arr.	,,	10.0 ,,	Fri.	7.0 A.M.
	dep.	,,	1.0 P.M.	,,	noon.
Pylos	arr.	,,	6.30 ,,	,,	4.45 P.M.
	dep.	Thurs.	3.0 ,,	Sat.	3.0 A.M.
Márathos		Calls.	arr.	,,	4.15 ,,
		...	dep.	,,	5.45 ,,
(H)agía Kyriaké		Calls in summer.		Calls in summer.	
Kyparissía	arr.	Thurs.	6.0 A.M.	Sat.	7.30 ,,
	dep.	,,	7.0 ,,	,,	9.0 ,,
Katákolo(n)	arr.	,,	10.30 ,,	,,	12.30 P.M.
	dep.	,,	2.0 P.M.	,,	2.0 ,,
Zante	arr.	,,	5.0 ,,	,,	4.45 ,,
	dep.	Fri.	7.0 A.M.	Sun.	1.0 A.M.
Kyllene	arr.	,,	9.0 ,,	Calls in summer.	
	dep.	,,	9.30 ,,	,,	
Mesolongi(on)	arr.	,,	12.30 P.M.	Sun.	5.30 A.M.
	dep.	,,	1.30 ,,	,,	8.0 ,,
Patras	arr.	,,	3.30 ,,	,,	10.0 ,,
	dep.	,,	11.0 ,,	,,	noon.
Æ'gion		...	arr.	,,	2.30 P.M.
(*Vostitza*)		...	dep.	,,	3.0 ,,
Itéa		...	arr.	,,	6.30 ,,
		...	dep.	Mon.	2.0 A.M.
Corinth	arr.	Sat.	7.0 A.M.	,,	6.30 ,,

[1] Touching at Kythnos every week from April to October; and once a fortnight from November to March.
[2] The days vary.

4. CORINTH—GYTHEION—PEIRÆUS, &c.

		Hellenic.		[1] Πανελλήνιος.	
Corinth	dep.	Sat.	noon.	Fri.	noon.
Itéa		...	arr.	,,	4.30 P.M.
		...	dep.	Sat.	2.0 A.M.
Æ'gion		...	arr.	,,	4.30 ,,
		...	dep.	,,	5.0 ,,
Patras	arr.	Sat.	8.0 P.M.	,,	7.0 ,,
	dep.	Sun.	6.30 A.M.	,,	noon.
Mesolongi	arr.	,,	8.30 ,,	,,	2.0 P.M.
	dep.	,,	9.0 ,,	,,	4.0 ,,
Kyllene	arr.	,,	noon.	...	
	dep.	,,	3.0 P.M.	...	
Zante	arr.	,,	2.30 ,,	Sat.	8.30 P.M.
	dep.	Mon.[2]	6.0 A.M.	Sun.	5.0 A.M.
Katákolo(n)	arr.	,,	9.0 ,,	,,	7.45 ,,
	dep.	,,	11.0 ,,	,,	9.0 ,,
Kyparissía	arr.	,,	2.30 P.M.	,,	12.30 P.M.
	dep.	,,	3.0 ,,	,,	1.0 ,,
Márathos		...	arr.	,,	2.45 ,,
		...	dep.	,,	3.0 ,,
Pylos	arr.	Mon.	6.0 P.M.	,,	4.15 ,,
	dep.	,,	11.30 ,,	Mon.	1.0 A.M.
Kalamáta	arr.	Tues.	5.0 A.M.	,,	5.45 ,,
	dep.	,,	8.0 ,,	,,	8.0 ,,
Gýtheion	arr.	,,	3.0 P.M.	,,	3.0 P.M.
	dep.	,,	5.0 ,,	,,	4.0 ,,
Peiræus	arr.	Wed.	8.0 A.M.	Tues.	6.45 A.M.
	dep.	Thurs.	8.0 ,,	Mon., Wed., 8.0 P.M.	
Kea	arr.	,,	1.15 P.M.	...	
	dep.	,,	1.45 ,,	...	
Syra	arr.	,,	6.15 ,,	Tu., Th., 5.30 A.M.	

[1] The days vary.
[2] From May to September the steamer, instead of stopping for the night at Zante, will leave for Katákolon an hour after its arrival; and reaching that place on the same day (Sunday), will leave about 9 A.M. on Monday for Kyparissía.

5. SYRA—PEIRÆUS—NAUPLIA

		Hellenic.	
Syra	dep.	Mon.	7.0 A.M.
Kythnos[1]			
Kea	arr.	,,	11.30 ,,
	dep.	,,	noon.
Peiræus	arr.	,,	5.15 P.M.
	dep.	Tues.	6.30 A.M.
Æ'gina	arr.	,,	8.15 ,,
	dep.	,,	8.30 ,,
Poros	arr.	,,	10.45 ,,
	dep.	,,	11.0 ,,
Hydra	arr.	,,	12.15 P.M.
	dep.	,,	12.30 ,,
Spezzia	arr.	,,	2.15 ,,
	dep.	,,	2.30 ,,
Cheli(on)	arr.	,,	3.0 ,,
	dep.	,,	3.15 ,,
Astros	arr.	,,	5.30 ,,
	dep.	,,	5.45 ,,
Nauplia	arr.	,,	7.0 ,,

GULF OF CORINTH

7. CORINTH—PATRAS

		Hellenic.		Πανελλήνιος.	
Corinth	dep.	Sun.	midnight.	Sat.	noon.
Itéa	arr.	Mon.	5.0 A.M.	,,	4.30 P.M.
	dep.	,,	5.30 ,,	Sun.	4.30 A.M.
Galaxídi(on)	arr.	,,	6.0 ,,	,,	5.0 ,,
	dep.	,,	6.15 ,,	,,	5.15 ,,
Æ'gion	arr.	,,	8.45 ,,	,,	7.30 ,,
(*Vostitza*)	dep.	,,	9.0 ,,	,,	8.0 ,,
Náupaktos	arr.	,,	10.45 ,,	,,	9.30 ,,
	dep.	,,	11.0 ,,	,,	9.45 ,,
Patras	arr.	,,	12.15 P.M.	,,	11.0 ,,

[1] Calls once a week from April to the end of October, and once a fortnight from November to the end of March (old style).

6. NAUPLIA—HYDRA—ÆGINA— PEIRÆUS—SYRA

		Hellenic.	
Nauplia	dep.	Wed.	6.0 A.M.
Astros	arr.	,,	7.15 ,,
	dep.	,,	7.30 ,,
Cheli(on)	arr.	,,	9.45 ,,
	dep.	,,	10.0 ,,
Spezzia	arr.	,,	10.30 ,,
	dep.	,,	10.45 ,,
Hydra	arr.	,,	12.30 P.M.
	dep.	,,	12.45 ,,
Poros	arr.	,,	2.0 ,,
	dep.	,,	2.15 ,,
Æ'gina	arr.	,,	4.30 ,,
	dep.	,,	4.45 ,,
Peiræus	arr.	,,	6.30 ,,
	dep.	Sat.	7.30 A.M.
Kea (Keos)	arr.	,,	12.45 P.M.
	dep.	,,	1.0 ,,
Syra	arr.	,,	5.30 ,,

GULF OF CORINTH

8. PATRAS—CORINTH

		Hellenic.		Πανελλήνιος.	
Patras	dep.	Tues.	9.0 A.M.	Sat.	9.0 A.M.
Náupaktos	arr.	,,	10.15 ,,	,,	10.15 ,,
	dep.	,,	10.30 ,,	,,	10.30 ,,
Æ'gion	arr.	,,	12.15 P.M.	,,	noon.
(*Vostitza*)	dep.	,,	12.30 ,,	,,	12.30 P.M.
Galaxidi(on)	arr.	,,	3.0 ,,	,,	2.45 ,,
	dep.	,,	3.15 ,,	,,	3.0 ,,
Itéa	arr.	,,	3.45 ,,	,,	3.30 ,,
	dep.	,,	midnight.	Sun.	2.0 A.M.
Corinth	arr.	Wed.	5.0 A.M.	,,	6.0 ,,

9. CORINTH—BRINDISI

		Hellenic.			[1] Πανελλήνιος.
Corinth	dep.	Wed.	1.0	P.M.	...
Pátras	arr.	,,	9.0	,,	...
	dep.	,,	10.0	,,	..
Corfu	arr.	Thurs.	1.0	,,	...
	dep.	,,	4.0	,,	...
Brindisi	arr.	Fri.	5.0	A.M.	[1] In connexion with Italian Steamers.

IONIAN ISLANDS LINE

11. CORINTH—ZANTE—KEPHALLENIA—CORFU

		Hellenic.			[3] Πανελλήνιος.		
Corinth	dep.	Fri.	1.0	P.M.	Mon.	noon	
Patras	arr.	,,	9.30	,,	,,	7.30	A.M.
	dep.	,,	midnight.		Tues.	3.0	,,
Kyllene[2]	arr.	...			,,	7.15	,,
	dep.	...			,,	7.30	,,
Zante	arr.	Sat.	6.30	A.M.	,,	9.0	,,
	dep.	,,	9.0	,,	,,	10.0	,,
Kephallenía	arr.	...			,,	2.30	P.M.
	dep.	...			,,	4.0	,,
Lixouri	arr.	Sat.	1.0	P.M.	...		
Argostoli	dep.	,,	5.0	,,	...		
Paxos	arr.	Sun.	1.30	A.M.	...		
	dep.	,,	1.45	,,	...		
Corfu	arr.	,,	5.30	,,	Wed.	3.0	A.M.

[2] In summer only.   [3] The days vary.

10. BRINDISI—CORINTH

		Hellenic.		Πανελλήνιος.
Brindisi	dep.	Fri.	midnight.	In connexion with Italian Steamers.
Corfu	arr.	Sat.	1.0 P.M.	...
	dep.	,,	2.0 ,,	...
Patras	arr.	Sun.	5.0 A.M.	...
	dep.	,,	6.0 ,,	...
Corinth	arr.	,,	2.0 P.M.	...

IONIAN ISLANDS LINE

12. CORFU—KEPHALLENIA—ZANTE—CORINTH

		Hellenic.		² Πανελλήνιος.	
Corfu	dep.	Mon.	5.30 P.M.	Wed.	5.0 P.M.
Paxos	arr.	,,	9.15 ,,	...	
	dep.	,,	9.30 ,,	...	
Kephallenía	arr.	...		Thurs.	5.0 A.M.
	dep.	...		,,	6.0 ,,
Argostoli	arr.	Tues.	6.0 A.M.	...	
Lixouri	dep.	,,	7.30 ,,	...	
Zante	arr.	,, 10 or 11.30 ,,		,,	10.0 A.M.
	dep.	,, 11 or 12.30 P.M.		,,	10.30 ,,
Kyllene¹	arr.	...		,,	12.30 P.M.
	dep.	...		,,	12.45 ,,
Patras	arr.	Tues.	7.0 P.M.	,,	5.0 ,,
	dep.	,,	10.0 ,,	,,	9.0 ,,
Corinth	arr.	Wed.	6.30 A.M.	Fri.	5.0 A.M.

¹ In summer only.   ² The days vary.

13. CORINTH—PREVESA—KARVASARA

		Hellenic.			Πανελλήνιος.		
Corinth	dep.	Mon.	8.0	P.M.	Thurs. noon.		
Patras	arr.	Tues.	4.0	A.M.	,,	7.30	P.M.
	dep.	,,	6.0	,,	Fri.	5.0	A.M.
Mesolongi(on)	arr.	,,	8.0	,,	,,	7.0	,,
	dep.	,,	8.30	,,	,,	7.30	,,
Astakós	arr.	,,	12.15	P.M.	,,	11.0	,,
	dep.	,,	12.30	,,	,,	11.15	,,
Mýtika	arr.	,,	2.0	,,	,,	1.30	P.M.
	dep.	,,	2.15	,,	,,	1.45	,,
Zavérda	arr.	,,	3.15	,,	Calls in summer.		
	dep.	,,	3.30	,,			
Aléxandros	arr.	,,	4.30	,,	Fri.	3.30	P.M.
	dep.	,,	5.0	,,	,,	3.45	,,
Ithaca	arr.	,,	8.0	,,	,,	6.15	,,
	dep.	,,	midnight.		Sat.	1.0	A.M.
Leukás	arr.	Wed.	5.0	A.M.	,,	5.30	,,
	dep.	,,	6.0	,,	,,	6.0	,,
Prévesa	arr.	,,	7.0	,,	,,	7.0	,,
	dep.	,,	7.30	,,	,,	8.0	,,
Salaóra	arr.	,,	8.30	,,	,,	9.15	,,
	dep.	,,	9.0	,,	,,	9.30	,,
Vónitsa	arr.	,,	9.45	,,	,,	10.30	,,
	dep.	,,	10.0	,,	,,	10.45	,,
Menídi(on)	arr.	,,	11.30	,,	,,	12.30	P.M.
	dep.	,,	12.30	P.M.	,,	12.45	,,
Karvasará	arr.	,,	2.0	,,	,,	2.0	,,
		...	dep.		,,	2.15	,,
Prévesa		...	arr.		,,	4.45	,,
		...	dep.		,,	5.15	,,
Leukás		...	arr.		,,	6.15	,,
		...	dep.		,,	7.0	,,
Corfu		...	arr.		Sun.	2.0	A.M.

14. KARVASARA—PREVESA—CORINTH

			Hellenic.		Πανελλήνιος.		
Corfu			...	dep.	Mon.	8.0	P.M.
Leukás			...	arr.	Tues.	3.0	A.M.
			...	dep.	,,	5.0	,,
Prévesa			...	arr.	,,	6.0	,,
			...	dep.	,,	6.30	,,
Karvasará			...	arr.	,,	9.0	,,
	dep.	Sat.	3.0	A.M.	,,	9.15	,,
Menídi(on)	arr.	,,	4.30	,,	,,	10.30	,,
	dep.	,,	6.0	,,	,,	10.45	,,
Vónitsa	arr.	,,	7.30	,,	,,	12.30	P.M.
	dep.	,,	7.45	,,	,,	12.45	,,
Salaóra	arr.	,,	8.30	,,	,,	1.45	,,
	dep.	,,	8.45	,,	,,	2.0	,,
Prévesa	arr.	,,	9.45	,,	,,	3.15	,,
	dep.	,,	10.0	,,	,,	4.0	,,
Leukás	arr.	,,	11.0	,,	,,	5.0	,,
	dep.	,,	11.15	,,	,,	5.30	,,
Ithaca	arr.	,,	4.15	P.M.	,,	10.0	,,
	dep.	,,	4.30	,,	Wed.	2.30	A.M.
Aléxandros	arr.	,,	7.30	,,	,,	5.0	,,
	dep.	Sun.	6.30	A.M.	,,	5.15	,,
Zabérda	arr.	,,	7.30	,,	...		
	dep.	,,	7.45	,,	...		
Mýtika	arr.	,,	8.45	,,	Wed.	7.0	A.M.
	dep.	,,	9.0	,,	,,	7.15	,,
Astakós	arr.	,,	10.30	,,	,,	9.30	,,
	dep.	,,	10.45	,,	,,	9.46	,,
Mesolongi(on)	arr.	,,	2.30	P.M.	,,	1.15	P.M.
	dep.	,,	3.0	,,	,,	1.30	,,
Patras	arr.	,,	5.0	,,	,,	3.30	,,
	dep.	,,	10.0	,,	,,	10.0	,,
Corinth	arr.	Mon.	6.0	A.M.	Thurs.	5.30	A.M.

15. SYRA and PEIRÆUS to VOLO

		Hellenic.			[1] Πανελλήνιος.		
Syra	dep.	Tues.	7.0	P.M.	...		
Peiræus	arr.	Wed.	4.0	A.M.	...		
	dep.	,,	7.30	P.M.	Mon.	7.0	P.M.
Láurion		...	arr.		,,	11.0	,,
		...	dep.		,,	11.15	,,
Chalkís	arr.	Thurs.	6.0	A.M.	Tues.	6.0	A.M.
	dep.	,,	7.30	A.M.	,,	7.0	,,
Stylída		...	arr.		,,	1.30	P.M.
		...	dep.		,,	2.30	,,
Volo	arr.	,,	5.30	P.M.	,,	8.0	,,

16. VOLO to PEIRÆUS and SYRA

		Hellenic.			[1] Πανελλήνιος.		
Volo	dep.	Fri.	8.0	P.M.	Wed.	noon.	
Stylída		...	arr.		,,	5.30	P.M.
		...	dep.		,,	10.0	,,
Chalkís	arr.	Sat.	6.0	A.M.	Thurs.	4.30	A.M.
	dep.	,,	7.30	,,	,,	5.30	,,
Láurion		...	arr.		,,	12.15	P.M.
		...	dep.		,,	12.30	,,
Peiræus	arr.	,,	6.0	P.M.	,,	4.30	,,
	dep.	Sun.	8.0	,,	...		
Syra	arr.	Mon.	5.0	A.M.	...		

[1] The days vary.

17. SYRA—LAURION

		HELLENIC.			
Syra	dep.	Wed.	7.0 A.M.	Fri.	7.0 A.M.
Gaurion	arr.	,,	10.30 ,,	...	
	dep.	,,	11.0 ,,	...	
Kárystos	arr.	,,	1.30 P.M.	...	
	dep.	,,	2.0 ,,	...	
Láurion	arr.	,,	5.30 ,,	Fri.	12.30 P.M.
	dep.	Thurs.	8.0 P.M.	,,	1.30 ,,
Kárystos	arr.	,,	11.30 ,,	...	
	dep.	,,	noon.	...	
Gaurion	arr.	,,	2.30 P.M.	...	
	dep.	,,	3.0 ,,	...	
Syra	arr.	,,	6.30 ,,	Fri.	7.0 P.M.

HELLENIC COMPANY'S STEAMERS

ARRIVALS AT LAURION.

Sun.   9.30 P.M. from Peiræus.
Mon.   3.0 ,,   ,, Syra, Kythnos, Keos.
Mon.   9.30 P.M. from Eubœa.
Wed.   9.30 ,,   ,, Peiræus.
 ,,   5.30 ,,   ,, Gaurion, Karystos, and Syra.
Thurs. 11.30 A.M. from Peiræus.
Fri.   12.30 P.M. ,, Syra (direct).
Sat.   2.30 P.M. from Volo, Stylída, and Chalkís.

DEPARTURES FROM LAURION.

Sun.   10.0 P.M. for Eubœa, and Thessalonika.
Mon.   3.15 P.M. for Peiræus.
 ,,   9.45 ,,   ,,   ,,
Wed.   9.45 ,,   ,, Chalkís, Stylída, and Volo.
Thurs. 8.0 A.M. for Karystos, Gaurion, and Syra.
Thurs. 11.45 A.M. for Keos, Kythnos, and Syra.
Fri.   1.30 P.M. for Syra (direct).
Sat.   2.45 ,,   ,, Peiræus.

18. SYRA and PEIRÆUS to VOLO

		Hellenic.	Πανελλήνιος.	Goudé.
Syra	dep.	Sat. 7.0 P.M.	Fri. 8.0 P.M.	...
Peiræus	arr.	Sun. 4.30 A.M.	Sat. 5.30 A.M.	...
	dep.	,, 8.0 P.M.	Th. 7.0 P.M.	Tu.&Sa. 7.0 P.M.
Láurion		Calls. arr.	,, 11.0 ,,	,, ,, 10.30 ,,
		dep.	,, 11.15 ,,	,, ,, 11.0 ,,
Alivéri(on)	arr.	Mon. 5.30 A.M.	Fri. 3.45 A.M.	W.&Su. 4.0 A.M.
	dep.	,, 5.45 ,,	,, 4.0 ,,	,, ,, 4.30 ,,
Chalkís	arr.	,, 8.45 ,,	,, 6.45 ,,	,, ,, 7.0 ,,
	dep.	,, 10.0 ,,	,, 7.45 ,,	,, ,, 8.0 ,,
Limne	arr.	,, 12.45 P.M.	,, 10.15 ,,	,, ,, 10.30 ,,
	dep.	,, 1.0 ,,	,, 10.30 ,,	,, ,, 11.0 ,,
Atalante	arr.	,, 2.30 ,,	noon.	...
	dep.	,, 2.45 ,,	,, 12.15 P.M.	...
Ædēpsós		...	Calls in summer.	...
Stylída	arr.	,, 7.0 ,,	,, 4.15 P.M.	{ Wed. 2.30 P.M.; Sun. 2.0 ,,
	dep.	Tues. 2.30 A.M.	,, 5.0 ,,	{ Wed. 3.30 P.M.; Sun. 3.0 ,,
Ôreós	arr.	,, 5.45 ,,	,, 8.0 ,,	...
	dep.	,, 6.0 ,,	,, 8.15 ,,	...
Nea Mizéle	arr.	,, 8.0 ,,	...	...
	dep.	,, 8.15 ,,	...	...
Halmyrós (=Armyró)	arr.	,, 8.45 ,,	...	...
	dep.	,, 9.0 ,,	...	...
Volo	arr.	,, 10.30 ,,	,, 11.0 ,,	W. & Su. 8.0 P.M.

19. VOLO to PEIRÆUS and SYRA

		Hellenic.		Πανελλήνιος.		Goudé.
Volo	dep.	Tues.	2.30 P.M.	Sat.	12 noon.	Tu. 11.0 A.M.; Th. 11.0 ,,
Halmyrós	arr.	,,	4.0 ,,	,,	1.30 P.M.	Th. noon.
	dep.	,,	4.15 ,,	,,	1.45 ,,	,, 1.30 P.M.
Nea Mizéle	arr.	,,	4.45 ,,	...		...
	dep.	,,	5.0 ,,	...		...
Ôreós	arr.	,,	[1]7.0 ,,	,,	4.0 ,,	,, 3.30 ,,
	dep.	Wed.	2.0 A.M.	,,	4.15 ,,	,, 4.0 ,,
Stylída	arr.	,,	5.15 ,,	,,	7.15 ,,	Tu. 5.0 P.M.; Th. 8.0 ,,
	dep.	,,	6.30 ,,	,,	midnight.	Tu. 8.0 ,, Th. midnight.
Atalante	arr.	,,	10.45 ,,	Sun.	4.0 A.M.	...
	dep.	,,	11.0 ,,	,,	4.15 ,,	...
Limne	arr.	,,	12.30 ,,	,,	5.45 ,,	Tues. midnight.
	dep.	,,	12.45 ,,	,,	6.0 ,,	,, ,,
Chalkís	arr.	,,	3.30 ,,	,,	8.30 ,,	Wed. 4.0 A.M.; Fri. 6.0 ,,
	dep.	,,	4.30 ,,	,,	9.0 ,,	Wed. 6.0 ,, Fri. 6.30 ,,
Alivéri(on)	arr.	,,	7.30 ,,	,,	11.45 ,,	Wed. 8.30 ,, Fri. 9.0 ,,
	dep.	,,	7.45 ,,	,,	noon.	Wed. 9.0 ,, Fri. 9.30 ,,
Laurion			arr.	,,	4.30 P.M.	Wed. 1.0 P.M.; Fri. 2.0 ,,
			dep.	,,	4 45 ,,	Wed. 1.30 ,, Fri. 2.30 ,,
Peiræus	arr.	Thurs.	5.14 A.M.	,,	8.45 ,,	Wed. 5.0 ,, Fri. 6.0 ,,
	dep.	,,	7.0 P.M.	Thurs.	8.0 P.M.	...
Syra	arr.	Fri.	4.30 A.M.	Fri.	5.30 A.M.	...

[1] From February to November the steamer, after waiting 15 minutes at Ôreós, crosses over to Stylída, and stays there for the night. In the winter months, it stays either at Ôreós or Stylída, at the discretion of the Captain.

20. SYRA—TENOS—MYCONOS

			HELLENIC.	
Syra	dep.	Sun.	8.0	A.M.
Tenos	arr.	,,	9.30	,,
	dep.	,,	10.0	,,
Mýconos	arr.	,,	11.15	,,
	dep.	,,	2.0	P.M.
Tenos	arr.	,,	3.15	,,
	dep.	,,	4.0	..
Syra	arr.	,,	5.30	,,

22. SYRA and MELOS

			HELLENIC.	
Syra	dep.	Fri.	8.0	A.M.
Sériphos	arr.	,,	11.30	,,
	dep.	,,	11.45	,,
Siphnos	arr.	,,	1.45	P.M.
	dep.	,,	2.0	,,
Melos	arr.	,,	5.15	,,

24. SYRA—THERA (first week.)

			HELLENIC.	
Syra	dep.	Mon.	7.0	A.M.
Náousa	arr.	,,	10.0	,,
(*in Paros*)	dep.	,,	10.15	,,
Naxos	arr.	,,	11.30	,,
	dep.	,,	noon.	
Amorgós	arr.	,,	4.30	P.M.
	dep.	Tues.	12.30	A.M.
Théra	arr.	,,	5.0	,,
(*Santorin*)	dep.	,,	7.0	,,
Ios	arr.	,,	9.30	,,
	dep.	,,	9.45	,,
Naxos	arr.	,,	12.45	P.M.
	dep.	,,	1.15	,,
Náousa	arr.	,,	2.30	,,
	dep.	,,	2.45	,,
Syra	arr.	,,	5.45	,,

21. SYRA and ANDROS

		HELLENIC.	
Syra	dep.	Wed.	8.0 A.M.
Hysternia (*in Tenos*)		} calls.	
Korthi(on) (*in Andros*)		} calls.	
Andros	arr.	Wed.	11.45 A.M.
	dep.	,,	12.30 P.M.
Syra	arr.	,,	4.15 ,,

23. SYRA and MELOS

		HELLENIC.	
Melos	dep.	Sat.	6.0 A.M.
Siphnos	arr.	,,	9.15 ,,
	dep.	,,	9.30 ,,
Sériphos	arr.	,,	11.30 ,,
	dep.	,,	11.45 ,,
Syra	arr.	,,	3.15 P.M.

25. SYRA—THERA (second week)

		HELLENIC.	
Syra	dep.	Mon.	7.0 A.M.
Paroikía	arr.	,,	10.0 ,,
(*in Paros*)	dep.	,,	10.15 ,,
Naxos	arr.	,,	12.30 P.M.
	dep.	,,	1.0 ,,
Ios	arr.	,,	4.0 ,,
	dep.	,,	4.15 ,,
Théra	arr.	,,	6.45 ,,
(*Santorin*)	dep.	Tues.	1.0 A.M.
Amorgós	arr.	,,	5.30 ,,
	dep.	,,	6.0 ,,
Naxos	arr.	,,	10.30 ,,
	dep.	,,	11.0 ,,
Paroikía	arr.	,,	1.15 P.M.
	dep.	,,	1.30 ,,
Syra	arr.	,,	4.30 ,,

26. SYRA to SKYROS.

(Once a fortnight)

		HELLENIC.	
Syra	dep.	Wed.	midnight.
Gáurion in Andros.			Calls.
Karystos	arr.	Thurs.	5.30 A.M.
	dep.	,,	6.0 ,,
Kyme	arr.	,,	1.0 P.M.
	dep.	,,	1.30 ,,
Skyros	arr.	,,	4.30 ,,
	dep.	,,	10.30 ,,
Karystos	arr.	Fri.	6.30 A.M.
	dep.	,,	7.0 ,,
Gáurion in Andros.			Calls.
Syra	arr.	,,	12.30 P.M.

27. PREVESA—ANTIVARIS.

		HELLENIC.	
Prévesa	dep.	Wed.	3.0 P.M.
Leukás	arr.	,,	4.0 ,,
	dep.	Thurs.	1.30 A.M.
Parga	arr.	,,	5.30 ,,
	dep.	,,	6.0 ,,
Sagiáda	arr.	,,	9.30 ,,
	dep.	,,	10.0 ,,
Corfu	arr.	,,	11.30 ,,
	dep.	,,	2.0 P.M.
(H)ag. Saranta	arr.	,,	4.0 ,,
	dep.	,,	5.0 ,,
Aulón	arr.	Fri.	1.0 A.M.
	dep.	,,	8.0 ,,
Dyrrhachion	arr.	,,	3.0 P.M.
	dep.	Sat.	1.0 A.M.
Médoua	arr.	,,	5.30 ,,
	dep.	,,	7.30 ,,
Antivaris	arr.	,,	noon.

28. ANTIVARIS—PRÉVESA.

		HELLENIC.	
Antivaris	dep.	Sun.	5.30 A.M.
Médoua	arr.	,,	10.0 ,,
	dep.	,,	11.30 ,,
Dyrrhachion	arr.	,,	4.0 P.M.
	dep.	,,	10.0 ,,
Aulón	arr.	Mon.	5.0 A.M.
	dep.		6.30 ,,
(H)ag. Saranta	arr.	,,	2.30 P.M.
	dep.	,,	3.0 ,,
Corfu	arr.	,,	5.0 ,,
	dep.	Tues.	4.0 A.M.
Sagiáda	arr.	,,	5.30 ,,
	dep.	,,	6.0 ,,
Parga	arr.	,,	9.30 ,,
	dep.	,,	10.0 ,,
Leukás	arr.	,,	2.0 P.M.
	dep.	,,	2.30 ,,
Prévesa	arr.	,,	3.30 ,,

29. TRIESTE—PATRAS—SALONICA

		Every alternate	
Trieste	dep.	[1] Wed.	6.0 P.M.
Fiume	arr.	Thurs.	7.30 A.M.
	dep.	,,	3.0 P.M.
Corfu	arr.	Sat.	4.30 ,,
	dep.	,,	9.30 ,,
S. Maura	arr.	Sun.	5.0 A.M.
	dep.	,,	7.0 ,,
Patras	arr.	,,	5.0 P.M.
	dep.	Mon.	4.0 A.M.
Katakolo	arr.	,,	noon.
	dep.	,,	5.0 P.M.
Kalamata	arr.	Tues.	4.30 A.M.
	dep.	,,	3.0 P.M.
Peiræus	arr.	Wed.	noon.
	dep.	Thurs.	10.0 A.M.
Volo	arr.	Fri.	9.30 ,,
	dep.	,,	3.0 P.M.
Salonica	arr.	[2] Sat.	8.30 A.M.
	dep.	Sun.	10.0 ,,
Constantinople	arr.	Thurs.	10.30 ,,

		Every alternate	
Constantinople	dep.	[2] Sat.	2.0 P.M.
Salonica	arr.	Wed.	5.0 A.M.
	dep.	,,	6.0 P.M.
Volo	arr.	Thurs.	11.30 A.M.
	dep.	,,	6.30 P.M.
Peiræus	arr.	Fri.	6.0 ,,
	dep.	Sat.	8.0 A.M.
Kalamata	arr.	Sun.	5.0 ,,
	dep.	,,	6.0 P.M.
Katakolo	arr.	Mon.	5.0 A.M.
	dep.	,,	8.30 ,,
Patras	arr.	,,	4.30 P.M.
	dep.	Tues.	1.0 A.M.
S. Maura	arr.	,,	11.0 ,,
	dep.	,,	9.0 P.M.
Corfu	arr.	Wed.	4.30 A.M.
	dep.	,,	8.0 ,,
Fiume	arr.	Fri.	9.30 P.M.
	dep.	,,	5.0 P.M.
Trieste	arr.	[2] Sat.	6.30 A.M.

[1] March 2, 16, 30; April 13, 27; May 11, 25; June 8, 22 in 1887.
[2] March 12, 26; April 9, 23; May 7, 21; June 4, 18 in 1887.

30. TRIESTE and CONSTANTINOPLE

Trieste	dep.	Sat.	2.0	P.M.
Corfu	arr.	Mon.	4.0	,,
	dep.	,,	7.0	,,
Peiræus	arr.	Wed.	10.0	A.M.
	dep.	,,	6.0	P.M.
Constantinople	arr.	Fri.	7.0	A.M.

31. PEIRÆUS and SYRA

Peiræus	dep.	Wed.	9.0	P.M.
Syra	arr.	Thurs.	7.0	A.M.

32. PEIRÆUS and CRETE

Peiræus	dep.	Sun.	2.0	P.M.
Canea	arr.	Mon.	8.0	A.M.
	dep.	,,	noon.	
Rethymnos	arr.	.,	4.0	P.M.
	dep.	,,	7.0	,,
Candia	arr.	.,	midnight.	

33. TRIESTE and SMYRNA

Trieste [1]	dep.	Tues.	4.0	P.M.
Brindisi	dep.	Fri.	midnight.	
Corfu	arr.	Sat.	2.30	P.M.
	dep.	,,	9.30	,,
Argostoli	arr.	Sun.	10.30	A.M.
	dep.	,,	1.0	P.M.
Zante	arr.	,,	5.30	,,
	dep.	,,	11.0	,,
Cerigo	arr.	Mon.	7.0	,,
	dep.	,,	8.0	,,
Syra	arr.	Tues.	11.0	A.M.
	dep.	,,	8.0	P.M.
Peiræus	arr.	Wed.	6.0	A.M.
	dep.	,,	3.0	P.M.
Chios	arr.	Thurs.	8.0	A.M.
	dep.	,,	9.0	,,
Smyrna	arr.	,,	4.0	P.M.

[1] Stopping at either Fiume or Ancona in alternate weeks.

CONSTANTINOPLE and TRIESTE.

Constantinople	dep.	Fri.	5.0	P.M.
Peiræus	arr.	Sun.	6.0	A.M.
	dep.	,,	4.0	P.M.
Corfu	arr.	Tues.	7.0	A.M.
	dep.	,,	11.0	,,
Trieste	arr.	Thurs.	1.0	P.M.

SYRA and PEIRÆUS.

Syra	dep.	Sat.	8.0	P.M.
Peiræus	arr.	Sun.	6.0	A.M.

CRETE and PEIRÆUS.

Candia	dep.	Sun.	midnight.	
Rethymnos	arr.	Mon.	5.0	A.M.
	dep.	,,	10.0	,,
Canea	arr.	,,	2.0	P.M.
	dep.	Tues.	8.0	A.M.
Peiræus	arr.	Wed.	2.0	,,

SMYRNA and TRIESTE.

Smyrna	dep.	Sat.	11.0	A.M.
Chios	arr.	,,	6.0	P.M.
	dep.	,,	7.0	,,
Peiræus	arr.	Sun.	noon.	
	dep.	,,	9.0	P.M.
Syra	arr.	Mon.	7.0	A.M.
	dep.	,,	4.0	P.M.
Cerigo	arr.	Tues.	7.0	A.M.
	dep.	,,	8.0	,,
Zante	arr.	Wed.	4.0	A.M.
	dep.	,,	8.30	,,
Argostoli	arr.	,,	1.0	P.M.
	dep.	,,	4.0	,,
Corfu	arr.	Thurs.	5.0	A.M.
	dep.	,,	7.0	P.M.
Brindisi[1]	arr.	Fri.	9.30	A.M.
Trieste	arr.	Mon.	5.30	,,

[1] Stopping at either Fiume or Ancona in alternate weeks.

GREEK RAILWAYS

GREEK RAILWAYS.

34. PEIRÆUS—CORINTH—NAUPLIA

Peiræus	dep.	7.0 A.M.	12.40[1] P.M.	
Athens		7.35 ,,	1.15	,,
Eleusis		8.45 ,,	2.30	,,
Megara		9.30 ,,	3.15	,,
Kalamaki		10.48 .,	4.32	,,
Corinth	arr.	11 15 ,,	5.0	,,
Corinth	dep.	12.0[2] .,	...	
Nemea	arr.	1.52 P.M.	...	
Phykhtia (Mycenæ)		2.14 ,,	...	
Argos[3]	arr.	2.50 ,,	...	
	dep.	3.15 ,,	...	
Myli (Lerna)[3]	arr.	3.35 ,,	...	
Nauplia[3]	arr.	3.15 ,,	...	

35. CORINTH—KAMARI

Corinth	dep.	11.40[4] A.M.	5.20[4] P.M.
Kiato		12.33 P.M.	6.20 ,,
Xylokastro		1.15 ,,	7.5 ,,
Kamari	arr.	1.30 ,,	7.20 ,,

[1] Stopping at Hag. Ioannes (Rhente), Myli (near Athens), Ano-Liósia Kato-Liósia, Kalyvia, Kinéta, and Hag. Theodoros.
[2] Stopping at Hexamili, Athékia, Chiliamodi, Hag. Vasileion, and Koutsopódi.

34. NAUPLIA—CORINTH—PEIRÆUS

Nauplia[3]	dep.	12.10[4]	P.M.		
Myli (Lerna)[3]	dep.	12.10	,,		
Argos[3]	arr.	12.45	,,		
Phykhtia (Mycenæ)		1.15	,,		
Nemea		1.51	,,		
Corinth	arr.	3.30	,,	...	
Corinth	dep.	10.15	A.M.	4.10[4]	P.M.
Kalamaki	arr.	10.46	,,	4.35	,,
Megara		12.0	,,	5.50	,,
Eleusis		12.48	P.M.	6.38	,,
Athens		2.5	,,	8.5	,,
Peiræus	arr.	2.40	,,	8.25	,,

35. KAMARI—CORINTH

Kamari	dep.	7.30[4]	A.M.	1.45[4]	P.M.
Xylokastro		7.55	,,	2.10	,,
Kiato		8.35	,,	2.50	,,
Corinth	arr.	9.30	,,	3.40	,,

[3] Between Myli, Argos, and Nauplia there is a local train three times a day, stopping at Dalamanára, Tíryns, and Kephalári.
[4] Stopping at Perigiáli, Vracháte, Kokkóni, Véllo, Deminio, Melíssi, and Sykiá.

36. ATHENS and KEPHISIA

Fares:—dr. 1.50, 1.05, and .75. Return, *dr.* 2.40, 1.80, and 1.20.

Stations: — Athens, Patesia, Heracleion, Amarousion, and Kephisiá.

1st April to 1st June [1] } **Athens**, dep., 6, 8, 11 A.M.; 2, 3, 5, 7 P.M.
1st Sept. to 26th Oct. [1] } **Kephisiá**, dep., 7, 9 A.M.; noon; 3, 4, 6, 9 P.M.

Extra Trains on Sundays and Holidays.
Athens, dep., 10 A.M.; 4, 5, 9 P.M.
Kephisiá, dep., 11.10 A.M.; 5.10, 8, 10 P.M. (instead of 9 P.M.)

1st June to 1st Sept. [1]   **Athens**, dep., 5.30, 7.30, 10.30 A.M.; 3, 4, 5, 6, 8 P.M.
Kephisiá, dep., 6.30, 8.30, 11.30 A M.; 4.10, 5.10, 6.10, 8.10, 10 P.M.

Extra Trains on Sundays and Holidays.
Athens, dep., 9.30 A.M.; 7, 9, 10 P.M.
Kephisiá, dep., 10.40, 11.40 (instead of 11.30) A.M.; 7.10, 9.10, 10.10 (instead of 10) P.M., and midnight.

26th Oct. to 1st April. [1]   **Athens**, dep., 7, 11 A.M.; 1.30, 2.30, 5.30 P.M.
Kephisiá, dep., 8.15 A.M.; noon; 2.40, 4.40, 6.40 P.M.

Extra Trains on Sundays and Holidays.
Athens, dep., 9 A.M.; 3.30, 6.30 P.M.
Kephisiá, dep., 10 A.M.; 5.40, 8 P.M.

[1] Old style.

37. ATHENS and PEIRÆUS

Fares:—lept. 95 ; 60 ; and 50.   Return, *dr.* 1.60 ; 1.05 ; and *lept.* 85.   All trains stop at Phalerum.

Peiræus, dep. 5.35 ; 5.5 ; 6.35 A.M., and every half-hour at 5 and 35 minutes past the hour, till 8.35 P.M.; also at 9.35 ; 10.35 ; 11.35 P.M.

Athens, dep. 6.0 A.M., and every half-hour, until 8.0 P.M.; also at 9.0 ; 10.0 ; 11.0 P.M., and midnight.

38. ATHENS and LAURIUM

Fares:—dr. 7.35, 5.55, and 3.70.   Return, *dr.* 12.70, 9.50, and 6.35.

Stations:—Athens, Patesia, Herakleion, Chalandrí, Géraka, Kantzas, Liópesi, Koropí, Markopúlo, Kalyvia, Keratéa, Daskaleion, Thorikós, and Laurium.

23d April to 26th Oct. (*Old Style.*) { **Athens**, dep., 7.45 A.M., and 4.30 P.M. **Laurium**, dep., 6.10 A.M., and 5.0 P.M.

26th Oct. to 23d April (*Old Style.*) { **Athens**, dep., 8.35 A.M., and 3.40 P.M. **Laurium**, dep., 7.5 A.M., and 4.5 P.M.

On *Fridays*, express in connexion with steamer between Laurium and Syra :—
Athens, dep., 10.45 A.M.
Laurium, dep., 1.30 P.M.

39. KATAKOLO and PYRGOS (for Olympia)

Old Style. New Style.	Pyrgos to Katakolo.					
	A.M.	A.M.	A.M.	P.M.	P.M.	P.M.
O. Jan. 1 to March 31 *N.* ,, 13 to April 12	7.0	9.30		1.30	4.0	...
O. Apr. 1 to May 31 *N.* ,, 13 to June 12	6.30	9.30		2.0	4.30	...
O. June 1 to Sept. 30 *N.* ,, 13 to Oct. 12	5.30	7.30	10.0	2.0	4.0	6.30
O. Oct. 1 to Dec. 31 *N.* ,, 13 to Jan. 12	6.30	8.30	10.30	2.0	4.30	...

Old Style. New Style.	Katakolo to Pyrgos.					
	A.M.	A.M.	A.M.	P.M.	P.M.	P.M.
O. Jan. 1 to March 31 *N.* ,, 13 to April 12	8.0	11.30		3.0	5.30	...
O. April 1 to May 31 *N.* ,, 13 to June 12	8.0	11.30		3.30	6.0	...
O. June 1 to Sept. 30 *N.* ,, 13 to Oct. 12	6.30	9.0	11.30	3.0	5.30	8.0
O. Oct. 1 to Dec. 31 *N.* ,, 13 to Jan. 12	7.30	9.30	11.30	3.30	6.0	...

Time: Half an hour.
Fares (payable in paper):—First Class, *dr.* 1.35; Second, *dr.* 1.15; Third, *dr.* .85. Return, First Class, *dr.* 2.10; Second, *dr.* 1.80; Third, *dr.* 1.60.
Special Trains: either way, *dr.* 70; both ways, *dr.* 120.

40. VOLO and LARISSA

N.B.—The Time-Table of this Line is to be found in Hendschel's *Telegraph*.

Volo	dep.	...	7.30 A.M.	8.42 A.M.	...	5.17 P.M.
Velestino	arr.	...	8.17 ,,	9.27 ,,	...	6.4 ,,
Velestino	dep.	...	...	9.37 ,,	...	...
Phérsala	,,	...	...	12.0 ,,	3.59 P.M.	...
Sophádes	,,	...	...	1.2 P.M.	5.20 ,,	...
Karditza	,,	7.0 A.M.	...	1.50 ,,	6.0 ,,	...
Trikkala	,,	8.47 ,,	...	3.15 ,,	...	...
Kalambákka	arr.	9.45 ,,	...	4.5 ,,	...	...
Velestino	dep.	...	8.28 A.M.	...	...	6.14 P.M.
Schoular	,,	...	9.22 ,,	...	..	7.8 ,,
Larissa	arr.	...	9.55 ,,	...	...	7.41 ,,

Larissa	dep.	...	7.50 A.M.	...	5.36 P.M.	...
Schoular	,,	...	8.24 ,,	...	6.10 ,,	...
Velestino	arr.	...	9.17 ,,	...	7.3 ,,	...
Kalambákka	dep.	...	...	11.35 A.M.	...	5.15 P.M.
Trikkala	,,	...	...	12.38 ,,	...	6.31 ,,
Karditza	,,	6.15 A.M.	...	2.0 P.M.	...	8.0 ,,
Sophádes	,,	7.0 ,,	...	2.35 ,,	..	...
Phérsala	,,	8.16 ,,	...	3.42 ,,	...	...
Velestino	arr.	...	...	5.55 ,,	...	...
Velestino	dep.	...	9.28 A.M.	6.5 ,,	7.8 P.M.	...
Volo	arr.	...	10.15 ,,	6.50 ,,	7.55 ,,	...

www.ingramcontent.com/pod-product-compliance
Lightning Source LLC
Chambersburg PA
CBHW030818190426
43197CB00036B/595